BLACK CONSCIOUSNESS

HLUMELO BIKO

BLACK
CONSCIOUSNESS

A Love Story

Jonathan Ball Publishers
Johannesburg • Cape Town • London

Published in South Africa in 2021 by
JONATHAN BALL PUBLISHERS
A division of Media24 (Pty) Ltd
PO Box 33977
Jeppestown
2043

ISBN 978-1-77619-044-7
ebook ISBN 978-1-77619-045-4

www.jonathanball.co.za
www.twitter.com/JonathanBallPub
www.facebook.com/JonathanBallPublishers

Cover by Sean Robertson
Design and typesetting by Nazli Jacobs
Set in ITC Veljovich

This book is dedicated to those who, as children,
sacrificed their lives in the Soweto protests on 16 June 1976.
None of us would be free without you.

Contents

Introduction

I often think about how I am going to tell my children the story of their grandparents, the ups and downs of their relationship, and the tragic circumstances surrounding the death of the Black Consciousness Movement (BCM) and the birth of their father. At some point, all children learn that death is an abrupt conclusion to the journey of life, yet I dread the prospect of describing to them the mortifying details of the death of Steve Bantu Biko.

For Luthando Bantu Biko and Imani Mamphela Biko, the 1970s will probably seem like the distant past. Naturally, at their young age, they don't have a sense of who their grandfather really was and what it was about his life that made it well lived. However, in six years for Luthando and 18 years for newborn Imani, they will reach adulthood and no doubt begin to ask some of the questions that led me to write this book.

Why didn't their grandparents get an opportunity to enjoy the freedom they fought so very hard for? What impulses caused their grandfather and his many colleagues to launch the BCM? What did he originally mean by the term 'Black Consciousness'?

I suspect they will also want to know what happened to Black Consciousness in the 21st century. Why are relationships between people still colour-coded in South Africa? Is this colour-coding the reason why social relationships seem to be deteriorating so badly? Furthermore, why is their grandparents' original vision for this country so radically different from the country we live in today? Given the socio-economic circumstances that most South Africans face, was their grandfather's death worthwhile?

These are questions that all South Africans should be asking.

In some way or another, we are all beneficiaries of the BCM. Without Black Consciousness, we would still refer to black people in South Africa as 'non-whites'. We would have neither the language nor the inclination to articulate the patronising behaviour some whites display in their feeble attempts to help black people living in material poverty. We might also have agreed to a post-apartheid dispensation that retained the demeaning concept of 'homelands'. Most importantly, black people would find it even more difficult than they currently do to express and harness their self-love.

I am a child of the Black Consciousness Movement in both a physical and a spiritual sense. I am privileged to be the product of my parents' uncompleted union. As with all South Africans born in the 1970s, I have been both blessed and cursed to grow up in the dusk of the movement, when its light shone the brightest and then rapidly faded into the violent darkness of the 1980s. I grew up in a family that has always tried to live the principles of Black Consciousness, and, like my siblings, I have been conscientised through the presence in my life of many of the founding members of the BCM. I am fortunate that I can rely on the wisdom and working memories of these individuals to help answer the challenging questions raised above.

Anyone who has met one of these extraordinary Black Consciousness leaders – for all of them were (and are) leaders in their own right – will feel they have interacted with spiritually and emotionally complete people who share a secret. In speaking to these heroes and heroines over the years, I have discovered that their shared secret was an intense love of self, and of others. This self-love was a source of energy that was used to propel a movement towards the goal of building a free nation. To have loved as they loved, despite the apartheid government's attempts to humiliate, demean and intimidate them, is one of the greatest achievements one can hope for in life.

We tend to equate love with soft emotions and intangible actions. This is not the type of love I am referring to. This love, or self-love, was an emotional and intuitive construct directly the opposite of what apartheid attempted to create among black South Africans. The architect of apartheid, Hendrik Verwoerd, imagined an outcome that would see black people hate themselves and what they saw of themselves in each other. In Verwoerd's vision, this self-hate would translate into a future where indigenous people would enslave themselves to the idea of white superiority. For Verwoerd to be successful, indigenous South Africans had to imprison themselves, to be forever classified within a racial category laced with the idea of inferiority.

Black Consciousness challenged Verwoerd's vision of the basis for white superiority over indigenous South Africans. In fact, the BCM argued that given the moral deficiencies of white right-wing racists and the moral complicity of white liberals, only black people held the moral high ground necessary to set the tone for what the new South Africa should look like.

The founders of the BCM had an indomitable spirit that rejected any restrictions on its right to full expression. Central to the BCM leaders' experience of self-love was an aversion to the oppression of any individual South African's spirit. This instinct was embedded in them at a young age when each of them answered, separately at first, the call to fight against apartheid oppression in both its petty and its grand manifestations.

They found the courage to start the fight against discrimination in their own communities and at institutions of learning. This enabled them to espouse a moral standard that many South Africans felt compelled to meet. They built up what Malcolm X described as an 'internal restraint' against the learnt instinct to submit to white people. Popularising this internal restraint is the ultimate legacy of the BCM; without it, we would be living in a very different country.

All countries have citizens who love one another and their nation. What Black Consciousness gave its adherents was a deep sense of human connectedness and the awareness of the individual's capacity for change based on self-knowledge and pride in the preservation of the dignity of all men and women. This gift is one that still helps people today to find a way to live in peace in a country where so many have so little in the midst of abundant material wealth for a few.

Self-worth is what many South Africans have continued to bank on despite the attempts by some, in both business and government, to bankrupt their country. That this sense of self-worth survived the brutal psychosocial onslaught of the apartheid era is part of the legacy of Black Consciousness.

South Africans, like people all over the world, tend to idealise people who commit great acts of courage. We attribute to our heroes and heroines traits that we convince ourselves are unavailable to us. Our heroes therefore seem larger than life, and it is easy to turn them into legends.

The problem with this is that it creates distance between us and those we admire, which can make us think that it must be difficult to follow their lead. This distance can create an excuse for us not to live courageously.

We may not all have access to the examples set by some of the most courageous people walking this planet, but we can overcome the distance between us and them every time we share in their documented wisdom. This will allow us to internalise the spirit of freedom, expressed most loudly on 16 June 1976.

There is an obligation on all of us to make their story part of our and our children's consciousness. When we do this, we will discover that these Black Consciousness leaders are just like us. The young people behind the BCM were ordinary people, most of whom came from humble beginnings. They were not perfect, and had faults, weaknesses and personal struggles, as we all do.

In their struggle to free their country, these young men and women were driven by the courage of their convictions and their sense of what was right and what was wrong. They were hardened by the pressure they felt to fight a form of tyranny that was as much psychological as it was physical.

They distinguished themselves by creating lasting human connections in communities where they previously didn't have any direct relationships. They were shaped by these human connections and were guided by them to fight to the bitter end for the material freedom they knew had to accompany the spiritual freedom they had attained.

I hope that you will learn as much from their story as I have. It is one of the greatest untold love stories. It is a love story not only of two individuals – Steve Biko and Mamphela Ramphele – but also of thousands of young South Africans who, by learning how to love themselves, set a new standard for how to love each other. This love story starts in townships and villages scattered around the country and climaxes, in tragic Shakespearean fashion, at a funeral held in eQonce (formerly King William's Town) on 25 September 1977.

My wish is that when you put this book down, you will understand how self-love and a love for your fellow human beings are like super powers that will allow you to invert what is scarce and what is abundant in life. As it did for the BCM leaders, time will teach us to cherish the abundant things that are nonmaterial in nature. We need to recognise the spiritual poverty suffered by many South Africans today who live with excess material abundance, which often manifests in the abuse of power, in the abuse of drugs and alcohol, or in an intense sense of loneliness. This is the price of pursuing money at all costs.

I hope you will appreciate how some of those who are born into difficult life circumstances compound their difficulties by embracing the narrative that they are poor. Being materially poor should not be a permanent state of being. I trust that the emotional and psychological tools used by the 15 young people at the heart of this love story will be useful in helping those who feel overwhelmed by material poverty. Benchmarking our lives against material wealth obscures the abundance of nonmaterial social capital that we can all freely tap into.

It is critical to create a shared understanding that this inversion of what is scarce and what is abundant can only take place in an environment in which we embrace self-love and self-reliance, value the importance of family – beyond the construct of the nuclear family – and try to restore complementary Black Consciousness programmes in our own communities.

If I succeed in my job as an author and as a parent, my son and daughter will grow up knowing what a powerful tool self-love is in releasing our natural capacity for empathy. As citizens of South Africa we need to use this empathy to build a nation that embraces the knowledge of how trivial the differences are between us as human beings, while recognising the critical importance of bridging the material divides that our past has bestowed on us.

Inspiring urgent action from this shared understanding is the most important task we as parents and citizens can take on. This is the only way to ensure a future for our children that will bring wellbeing, sustainable livelihoods, safety, security, empowerment and shared opportunities.

Steve Biko and Mamphela Ramphele, East London, 1977.
(*Daily Dispatch*/Arena Holdings Archives)

1

Living with loss

On an overcast morning at the beginning of the summer of 2019, I hurriedly left my home in Cape Town at 5 am, caught an Uber and headed to the airport. As I settled into my seat on the plane, I recognised several passengers who were joining me on the journey to East London. Matters that had seemed urgent and important a few days ago now faded into the background. My beloved Aunt Nobandile Biko had passed away ten days earlier, at the age of 70.

At the time of her death she lived in Cape Town, but, in keeping with family custom, she wanted to be buried next to her brother, Steve, in eQonce. I had attended the memorial service earlier that week, yet for reasons that took me some time to understand, it had still not sunk in that Aunt Bandi was no more. I felt completely at sea after losing my aunt, as she was my last direct connection to my father. She had been a constant source of family oral history and inside jokes and insights; she had created a sense of continuity with my father's life that had suddenly come to an end.

A few weeks before her untimely death, Aunt Bandi had told me how she had never got over the pain of losing Bantu Biko at such an early age. On that occasion we had held, in the Biko tradition, what we jokingly call a 'meat meeting'. This is where we share a good bottle of wine or two over some braaied meat and plenty of boisterous conversation. Aunt Bandi was particularly reflective that night, and had regaled me with stories about my parents that, at the age of 41, I was hearing for the first time.

She was always so proud of the fact that my parents were alike in that they never let themselves be defined by how much money they had in their pockets or what someone thought of them. Her favourite stories were about how my father had stood up to policemen or other figures of authority who had tried to bully him or people around him. He would be polite in telling them what line they couldn't cross while firmly assuring them of his ability to match the level of violence they were threatening to inflict. It was the calm delivery of these warnings that shook the confidence of would-be bullies.

In retelling these stories, Aunt Bandi communicated what she thought was a missing trait in many young black South Africans she had encountered since the end of apartheid: she couldn't get over how unwilling they were to stand up for themselves against clear abuses of power.

My ponderings on my last meeting with my aunt were interrupted as we approached East London. Because of low cloud cover, it took the pilot three attempts to put the plane on the tarmac. The first two were abandoned at the last second when, in both instances, the pilot realised he was flying over buildings instead of the runway. I was quite relieved when I could finally feel the ground beneath my feet again, and was soon in a taxi on my way to eQonce.

My driver was a chatty Afrikaner gentleman called Frikkie who had lived in Pretoria for most of his life but had in recent years moved to the Eastern Cape. He had married a Xhosa woman and wholly embraced the Eastern Cape version of African culture. Children had been born of the union, and Frikkie told me about the stares his multi-ethnic family would get from racists whenever they were in a shopping mall.

Frikkie's 'kill them with kindness' approach to these people initially struck me as a mature and conscious approach to his new life. However, the longer we spoke, the more I got the sense that Frikkie carried his marriage as a badge of honour for which he craved acknowledgement. He seemed slightly uncomfortable with the nonchalant way most people reacted. What he was experiencing is something that people who spend time in the Eastern Cape quickly learn: it takes a lot to draw praise from amaXhosa. They will certainly not hand out brownie points simply because you have fallen in love with one of their own.

Eastern Cape people are genuinely of the salt-of-the-earth variety. There is something special about this part of the world, where rural meets urban and township meets suburb without the harsh boundaries set up in the rest of the country. The rolling hills that are so typical of the region's topography are as gentle as the even-keeled approach to life of its inhabitants. This relaxed, easy-going culture masks a stubborn determination, displayed by the amaXhosa throughout the Eastern Cape's long history of resistance to any assault on their way of life.

Aunt Bandi was born on 21 February 1949, just a year after the National Party came to power. In many ways, her life was emblematic of the professional and emotional cost of apartheid borne by black families across the country. She lost her father at a young age to an avoidable death caused by a disease that was not treated because he was black. Aunt Bandi would lose one of her brothers because of apartheid state-sponsored terrorism, and another because of alcohol abuse, which was an almost inevitable consequence of the lack of intellectual stimulation in the township he had to live in. She also lost a husband because of mental illness triggered by trauma suffered when he was tortured by the security police.

My aunt was systematically denied education opportunities from early in life, and only through sheer tenacity and will-power was she able to complete her graduate qualification, focusing on youth leadership development, in the United Kingdom. After receiving her master's degree in the early 2000s, she returned to South Africa. However, her unwillingness to yield to white superiority made it difficult for her to get or keep a job. When she died, she was working as an estate agent, severely underpaid and hopelessly underappreciated.

Aunt Bandi found comfort in her ever-growing faith in God. This allowed her to bring a serene and jovial demeanour to any interaction. The life I had come to eQonce to celebrate was characterised by a series of triumphs over adversity.

When I arrived at the church, the ceremony was already under way. The choir was singing at the high-octane levels African choristers reach so effortlessly. The priest gave a moving sermon that displayed both his grasp of scripture and his in-depth knowledge of Aunt Bandi's life. My elder brother Nkosinathi was expertly playing the role of family patriarch, comforting those who needed it with a hug and coordinating the efforts of those who were composed enough to perform key tasks. Nkosinathi has always performed this role well; when we were growing up, it meant that my siblings Samora, Malusi, Bulie and I had the luxury of acting our age. The cost to Nkosinathi was that he did not have much of an opportunity just to be a child or a goofy teenager.

African funerals serve a social purpose that is not well understood in the Western world. A funeral is an occasion to both mourn together and rejuvenate one another with love. Through their presence at a funeral, family and friends get to display their solidarity anew. For this reason, Uncle Barney Pityana's face was one that I had expected to see at Aunt Bandi's funeral but didn't. Even before I heard that he had had an emergency in Gqeberha (formerly Port Elizabeth) on the same day as the funeral, I knew there had to be a logical explanation for his absence. But his younger brother, Uncle Sipho Pityana, was there, and the two of us spent a few moments catching up.

Despite our family's shock and sadness that day, we successfully controlled our emotions. Our family is made up of a complicated web of different nuclei connected through nodes of children born within and outside marriage, adopted cousins and family friends who are so close that many of the children don't know to distinguish them from their so-called blood family. The ease with which our family connects and supports each other on such occasions always astounds me. The family has an efficient, almost business-like approach to laying loved ones to rest. Everyone knows what their role is, and puts aside whatever personal issues they may have, taking pride in collectively succeeding in the fulfilment of their obligations.

Tensions between various family members were kept at bay and would only be visible to the keenest of observers. As senior members of the family died, those who felt they had scores to settle sometimes, sadly, tried to use younger members of the family as proxies for a turf war. Under the watchful eye of our paternal grandmother, Mamcete, these tensions were not allowed to flare up.

Mamcete had had two children before she married my grand-father Mzingaye, but she seamlessly integrated them into their family and created an environment in which they felt supported and loved. Mamcete did not believe in contrived family boundaries. To her, family was family, finish and *klaar*. She instilled a strong values-based family culture that all of us still treasure to this day.

For many decades, the Biko family has had to deal with losing loved ones at an early age. First, my grandfather Mzingaye died when my father was only four years old. A respected King William's Town policeman who was studying to be a lawyer, Biko senior did not live long enough to taste the fruits of his labours. Mzingaye upheld strong African traditions that continue to guide the way our family performs our rite-of-passage ceremonies, weddings and funerals. Our family lives by his dignified, holistic moral code, which implores us to treat all people we come across with respect, and to carry an unapologetic expectation that this respect is mutual.

The job of raising his children fell to Mamcete, who at the time was working as a cook at Grey Provincial Hospital. Despite her cook's salary, she made sure that all her children got an education and graduated from high school. My father went to university to study medicine; his sister Bukelwa trained as a nurse; his brother, Khaya, worked as a clerk in a legal firm; and, as previously noted, Bandi went on to earn a master's degree from a university in London.

My very beautiful Aunt Bukelwa died of a heart attack in 1975, leaving her siblings with another gap in the family tree. By the time she passed away she was a senior nurse who had worked at King Dinuzulu Hospital in then Natal before transferring to Tower

Psychiatric Hospital at Fort Beaufort, in the then eastern Cape Province. Aunt Bandi explained that Aunt Bukelwa often gave my father much-needed pocket money, which complemented his full scholarship and allowed him to live a semblance of a normal student life throughout his time at medical school in Durban. According to Aunt Bandi, one of his bitter regrets was that he was not able to repay his sister before her death.

I suspect Aunt Bukelwa's death brought my father and Aunt Bandi even closer. The two of them had always got along while growing up, but he grew even more protective of her as time went by. They shared a wicked sense of humour, a keen insight into what makes people tick, and the capacity to take painful events in their stride. They both loved intensely, often putting their own needs aside to make others feel comfortable.

Their elder brother, Khaya, died a little more than 15 years ago. He cared deeply for my father and did not feel it necessary to try and compete with his gifted and more famous younger brother. Uncle Khaya was held back by his love of alcohol, but if it hadn't been for that, he might have been an intellectual giant within the Pan Africanist Congress (PAC). He had a sharp, clear mind, an amazing memory for detail and excellent comedic timing that made you hang on his every word when he told a story. He had a deep wisdom that allowed him to calmly and objectively analyse political events. Until the end of his life, Uncle Khaya resented white people for their imperial and colonial exploits in Africa. Within the family he popularised the expression 'abelungu ngo-damn' (loosely translated, damn white people).

Throughout her life, Aunt Bandi showed some of the typical characteristics of a younger sibling. She needed and wanted constant love and reassurance, and she loved being cared for and spoilt. She revelled in the attention of others, and was fiercely loyal to her friends and family. Aunt Bandi was the least judgemental person I have known. You could tell her anything and she would always smile and reply, 'Nyani toto?' (Really, sweetheart?). Perhaps this is because her elder siblings loved and protected her regardless of her ups and downs, often even getting a kick out of Aunt Bandi's petulance.

In the late 1960s, Aunt Bandi married a dapper, attractive man called Mxolisi Mvovo. Together with their two children, Phumzile and Thandeka, the Mvovos first lived in Walmer township in Port Elizabeth (today Gqeberha). My father remained close to all his siblings, even after he left for boarding school and later for university, and he kept a special eye out for Aunt Bandi, making positive interventions in her life when he could.

At my father's encouragement, Aunt Bandi moved to Durban in the early 1970s to do a secretarial course. He introduced her to my mother Mamphela Ramphele, when she was doing her fourth year of medical studies at the University of Natal. My parents made sure that the warden of the Alan Taylor Residence, where my mother lived as a student, looked the other way and allowed Aunt Bandi to stay in my mother's room. It was the start of a 50-year friendship between the two women.

Even though she was the younger sibling, Aunt Bandi played an important role in my father's love life. She was the glue in the relationship between my mother and father. The three of them had separate but symbiotic relationships, which made it easy for my mother to integrate with my father's side of the family.

After completing her course in Durban, Aunt Bandi got a secretarial job at the Border Council of Churches in King William's Town. This led the Mvovos to move to the nearby Dimbaza township. When my mother moved to Mount Coke Hospital in 1974, and later to Zinyoka village to establish and run the Zanempilo Community Health Centre, the opportunity arose to re-establish their friendship.

My father's death in 1977 left Aunt Bandi and my mother heart-broken and with a permanent void that would never be filled. The person they loved most in life had been taken away from them at a moment when both, for very different reasons, desperately needed him. For both women, no other man would ever measure up to the Bantu they had known and loved.

The highly successful and fulfilling lives they both managed to live, despite this and other tragedies, testify to their resilience and are ultimately also a measure of their spirituality. This resilience is a hallmark of our extended family. Tragedies and joys, births and deaths – all were made easier by our undying support for one another.

I believe the greater Biko family's experience with loss makes us appreciate life differently than most people. We live and love just that little bit harder, because experience has taught us how fleeting life is. As a result many of us, even the older members of the family, have a capacity to party like there is no tomorrow. For the same reason, we do not easily allow new people into our lives. We take our time to get to know and trust people, and we favour high-quality relationships over a large number of lesser friendships. These are some of the wounds caused by apartheid and hidden by the glare of our rainbow nation.

Living with loss, and learning to love ourselves and one another, is made more difficult by the challenge of finding ways to forgive without there being reciprocal contrition. We all wrestle with the inherent contradiction of being a family torn apart by loss but morally compelled to forgive. It is not surprising that despite our reconciliation with white South Africans, on many occasions we find ourselves returning to Uncle Khaya's phrase, 'abelungu ngo-damn'. At our last meeting, Aunt Bandi said this phrase to me several times as we considered how difficult it was for indigenous South Africans to make an honest living in a country still controlled by an entrenched white-supremacist network.

Our entire family was shocked at Aunt Bandi's sudden death, and also that she was alone when she passed away. It left all of us with a sense of shame that this beautiful soul died alone in her townhouse, especially given how much she had loved the human connection. She had constantly sought out our company and was happiest when she was with family, telling stories over a meal. Once she found someone to share time with, she could talk into the wee hours of the morning.

Aunt Bandi was energised by humour; her whole face would light up when she was being told a story that she knew would end in laughter. This effervescence is a common Biko trait.

I wish we could have been there with her on her dying day. Today, two years after her death, we are all still finding ways to pick up the pieces and live with our loss. Because of her passing, the family at least found occasion to reconnect before COVID-19 introduced a new, socially distanced reality to our world.

2

An oasis of excellence

My father grew up in King William's Town as a boisterous, mischievous child who was popular among his friends thanks to his great sense of humour. As a child, he could usually be spotted playing barefoot outside, blissfully lost in a make-believe world that kept him entertained.

From the time he started at Charles Morgan Primary School, he was always at or close to the top of his class and he was promoted straight from Standard 1 (Grade 3) to Standard 3 (Grade 5). He continued to perform well at Forbes Secondary School, showing for the first time a flair for sports and debating.

In 1963 he was accepted at the legendary Lovedale College, a mission school in Alice, about 230 kilometres northeast of Gqeberha. This was where he first met a young Barney Pityana. It was the beginning of a friendship that would change the course of South African history. The Pityanas have always been such close family friends that I grew up believing they were relatives. It might be because their upbringing was so similar to the Bikos that the two families share an intimate familiarity.

Uncle Barney's mother, Ruth Nomfimfi Pityana, started her working life as a domestic worker, but studied part-time to become a nurse. She ended up living in New Brighton and working at Livingstone Hospital. Makhulu Ruth went on to play an important role in the provincial public health system by founding a nursing college at Cecilia Makiwane Hospital in Mdantsane, and also helping to create the first home for the aged in Zwide township.

Besides Barney, Makhulu Ruth had two other sons, Sipho and Lizo, whom she raised in a loving household where the power of independent thinking was valued. Uncle Barney was always extremely bright, exceptionally diligent in his studies and serious about his responsibilities. These traits made him a natural leader. After excelling at primary school, Uncle Barney, then 15, was awarded the prestigious Andrew Smith Scholarship and fulfilled his childhood ambition when he was sent to high school at Lovedale College.

Lovedale, set up by the Glasgow Missionary Society, had been around for more than 135 years by the time Uncle Barney arrived there. Built in the light-grey brick typical of ecclesiastical architecture at the time, the school, alongside the University College of Fort Hare (today the University of Fort Hare), was an oasis of excellence in the small town of Alice. Uncle Barney remembers the culture in Alice at this time as highly intellectual and intensely political. The school was filled with students who were the best and brightest in their communities. He quickly established a reputation among his peers by constantly topping the class in almost all his subjects.

Given that Lovedale's alumni includes the likes of Oliver Tambo, Nelson Mandela, ZK Matthews and Govan Mbeki, the school had a very deep African National Congress (ANC) culture. Shortly after he arrived at Lovedale, Uncle Barney found himself in an underground ANC cell group where he was exposed to the political history of the party, its approach to resistance and how it thought about the struggle for independence.

His intellectual curiosity drove him to engage more deeply with this culture, allowing him to become familiar with the ideas driving ANC debates at the time. Uncle Barney remembers that on several occasions Chris Hani, another Lovedale alumnus, came to campus to lecture the group on the Freedom Charter. This thrilling intellectual environment awakened in him a commitment to the liberation of the people of South Africa.

In the space of a few years, Lovedale was the place of learning for Thabo Mbeki, Steve Biko and Barney Pityana. The future President Mbeki was just over four years older than my father and three years Uncle Barney's senior. Mbeki and Pityana would become acquainted through their political work in the ANC's student-engagement activities. Mbeki worked closely with Uncle Barney in an organisation called the African Students' Association, established in 1961 as an alternative youth structure by the ANC. After its banning in 1960, the ANC had to find ways to remain relevant in the daily lives of South African people, and students were a natural constituency.

That Uncle Barney and President Mbeki would go on to have a long-lasting friendship serves as a historical teaser for the relationship that was not to be between Mbeki and my father. Mbeki was expelled from Lovedale in 1959 because of his first known political act, when he led student protests against the unjust expulsion of a fellow student. Like many legendary figures before and after him at the school, Lovedale helped to shape, and was shaped by, Thabo Mbeki.

It should come as no surprise that these African giants all went to Lovedale. The school's reputation for high-quality education attracted talented students from all over the eastern Cape and beyond. Eager to give their children the best chance at a successful future, African parents scraped together whatever resources they had to send their children to Lovedale and other mission schools.

Like many black parents of the time, Mamcete did not have the money to send her son to further his education at Lovedale. During the apartheid era, the education of most township children ended at Standard 8 (Grade 10). Under normal circumstances, someone like my father would then have had to become a teacher, fireman or policeman. Fortunately for Steve Biko, Mamcete was a diligent parishioner of the Anglican church. One of the priests at her church put her in touch with an Anglican priest by the name of Father Aelred Stubbs, who was a member of the Community of the Resurrection based in Alice. (The community's headquarters in South Africa was at St Peter's Seminary in Rosettenville, Johannesburg. It was headed by Father Trevor Huddleston, who was responsible for providing a young Hugh Masekela with a trumpet and for encouraging him to make the most of his musical talent.) Father Stubbs was on the teaching staff of the Federal Theological Seminary, which produced such luminaries as Njongonkulu Ndungane and Sabelo Ntwasa. It was Father Stubbs who helped arrange a scholarship for my father to attend Lovedale.

Since Uncle Barney had already been at Lovedale for three years, he was tasked with orienting my father on his first day at school. He and Steve were assigned a desk to share. Uncle Barney recalls how my father, shockingly for a new boy from the township, outperformed all the other students in his class in the first June exams at Lovedale, when he came top in the class.

For Barney Pityana, this was a sign that Steve was someone who deserved his respect. The two would become closer and closer as the year went by.

By the time my father arrived at Lovedale in 1963, the college was beginning to lose its administrative independence as the white-minority government was determined to put in place measures to erode the quality of mission-school teaching. A new Afrikaans-speaking vice-chancellor had been appointed, bringing with him new Afrikaans-speaking teachers who did not have the same academic background as their predecessors.

As a result, the standard of education dropped sharply, and students such as Barney Pityana, who knew the former high academic standards of Lovedale, began to launch protest actions against the new regime. They refused to attend classes and participate in normal student activities until their demands for the reinstatement of the old standards were met. Police were called to the campus and several of the troublemakers were rounded up and arrested. Though Uncle Barney was not surprised to be arrested, it surprised him that a new student like my father was also picked up.

My father was not the only Biko child at Lovedale; Khaya was there as well, and in 1963 was completing his final year of school. Uncle Khaya delighted in telling the story of how his activism within the PAC was responsible for getting him and my father kicked out of Lovedale. Uncle Khaya was arrested by the authorities for his suspected involvement in Poqo, the military wing of the PAC. Following Khaya's arrest, both he and my father were taken to King William's Town and interrogated. At the conclusion of this interrogation, Uncle Khaya was charged and given a two-year prison sentence, with 15 months suspended. My father, who was not charged, was excluded from Lovedale, as was Uncle Barney. My father was helped again by Father Stubbs, who arranged a scholarship to St Francis College at Mariannhill, outside Durban.

According to Uncle Khaya, before my father's exclusion from Lovedale he was a confident and opinionated rugby-playing boy who had no real interest in politics. Uncle Khaya claimed, probably correctly, that it was this seminal event in Steve Biko's life that led to his political awakening and the slow journey that would see him and Uncle Barney, and others, found the South African Students' Organisation (SASO). It was out of SASO that the BCM eventually flowed.

This was how Biko and Pityana were confronted, early in life, with the price of fighting against the system. At the time, the media coverage of the Rivonia Trial had created a political context that primed the two youngsters to become significant political actors. They were fortified and shaped by the stories of the great cost in personal freedom paid by the Rivonia defendants – Nelson Mandela, Arthur Goldreich, Andrew Mlangeni, James Kantor, Denis Goldberg, Harold Wolpe, Elias Motsoaledi and others – and witnessed on a personal level how virtue can lead to a loss of liberty. For all these reasons, Biko and Pityana found courage in the power of truth and resolved to pursue it to its logical conclusion – whatever the cost.

The cost of telling truth to power was initially steeper for Uncle Barney than for my father. After his expulsion, Uncle Barney found himself back in his home township of New Brighton, where he attended Newell High School, which was several notches below the quality of education he had enjoyed at Lovedale. Despite this setback, he focused his mind on his political activities. He established and led the local chapter of the African Students' Association, further integrating himself into ANC politics, and began seriously contemplating the idea of going into exile. However, on the day he was supposed to be picked up to cross the border, he had a change of heart and decided to finish his high-school studies and begin a law degree at Fort Hare.

Thanks to the injustice of his arrest at Lovedale and subsequent interrogation, my father was fully awakened politically, and began to come into his own. He was fortunate to find himself at another top-quality high school. At St Francis College he thrived both socially and academically, becoming the vice chair of the Literary and Debating Society. Intellectually and socially, he stood out even in comparison with other talented students such as Jeff Baqwa (elder brother of Selby Baqwa, who also matriculated at Mariannhill) and Charles Sibisi. Uncle Charles remembers my father as being an exceptional rugby player, while Jeff Baqwa once told me that he was taken aback by my father's great self-confidence.

The Roman Catholic nuns who made up the majority of the teaching staff at Mariannhill encouraged Steve Biko's inquisitive mind. They were not threatened when he asked deep questions touching on the foundations of their faith. They encouraged him to follow his analytical process of inquisition to its logical conclusion. These interactions built on Steve Biko's inherent confidence in his intellectual abilities. His daily contact with the nuns also allowed him to become comfortable in his skin among white figures of authority.

In December 1964 my father underwent the traditional rites of passage that all Xhosa men are expected to go through. This experience, and the Xhosa history his elders shared with him about Xhosa traditional leaders and their struggle to retain their people's autonomy and culture, must have added to his sense of purpose and duty to oppose oppression. The knowledge that his people were ably led by leaders such as King Hintsa, Chief Sandile and Chief Maqoma in legendary battles against colonial forces would have seared in the mind of the young Steve Biko a sense of reverence for what a unified resistance against oppression could achieve.

He returned to Mariannhill with a newfound inner resolve to not, under any circumstances, allow his dignity as a man to be trampled on. This, together with his natural protectiveness towards those weaker than himself, contributed to his steely determination when faced with danger of any sort. These were all important building blocks for the kind of self-love that was exceptional about, but not unique to, Steve Biko.

At the end of 1965, he wrote the following for the yearbook of his matric class: 'What do we take away with us from St Francis College? Besides having been prepared for the matriculation examinations, we have had the benefit of an all-round preparation for facing the world. Inter alia, I could mention the Debating Society, which has trained many of us in public speaking, and play-acting, which has revealed and developed potential histrionic talents in some of us. No less important is character-moulding and training in self-knowledge.'[1]

With this preparation as his educational background, my father left high school as a confident young man with dazzling public-speaking skills that would help him hone his greatest God-given strength – his mastery of the art of persuasion.

3

A lioness at the foot of the Soutpansberg

On the other side of the country, in the province known today as Limpopo, a young rural student named Mamphela Aletta Ramphele was impressing her teachers with her intellect and application. She grew up in a typical BaPedi household in Kranspoort, at the foot of the Soutpansberg.

Her family was a large, tight-knit nucleus of nine people, occasionally supplemented by various cousins and relatives. The household was run by a strong matriarch, Motsebore Ramphele, or Tsipu, as we liked to call her. Tsipu had to juggle her teaching job with the needs of her family, comprising her husband and seven children, which meant that she managed things in a military style. My mother and her siblings learnt from an early age how to work hard. Everyone had responsibilities, ranging from cooking, cleaning and hunting to tending to crops in the fields in summer, growing vegetables in the family garden and fetching water.

My maternal grandfather, Pitsi Ramphele, was the principal at Stephanus Hofmeyr Primary School in Kranspoort mission village. He was an introvert known for getting lost in his books. By all accounts, my grandfather carried himself with immense poise and prided himself on his upright character. This was fully displayed in the way he discharged his duties, with an old-fashioned fastidiousness. He combined this discipline with a naturally industrious nature, which made him a great provider for his extended family.

My grandfather's excellence as a teacher, and his belief in knowledge as the key to success, had earned him a great reputation, from when he first became a teacher at Malaka Matete Community School in the 1940s in his home district of Uitkyk. This reputation followed him to Kranspoort mission. My grandfather's long-standing friendship with his homeboy, Morena Ngoasheng, a local principal in the Uitkyk district, provided him with stimulating company during school holidays when the whole family visited his natal home. During these visits, my grandfather would invest time, effort and money in identifying young people in this area who would benefit from his support.

Moss Ngoasheng, the son of Morena, recalls grandfather Pitsi Ramphele being a frequent visitor to his home when he was growing up. Moss was himself a gifted student who went on to become an economic advisor to President Thabo Mbeki. To this day, Bra Moss retains fond memories of my grandfather. He once told me that he was inspired at a young age to develop a thirst for knowledge by conversations around the family dinner table when my grandfather, Pitsi, visited.

There are quite a few prominent individuals from that period who have kind words to say about both Pitsi and Tsipu. Mathews Phosa, a former leader of the Azanian People's Organisation (Azapo) and former ANC treasurer-general, who hails from the Blouberg district in a village near Uitkyk, attests to the fact that even in neighbouring villages, my grandparents earned a sterling reputation over their lifetime for reliability, kind-heartedness and service to the community.

My mother completed her primary education at Stephanus Hofmeyr Primary School under my grandfather's watchful eye. Thereafter she headed to boarding school, at Bethesda Normal College, for her secondary education. Mamphela survived the ordeal of poor-quality boarding-school food by rationing the provisions her mother taught her how to make before the start of each term: biscuits, rusks, biltong, dry morogo and mopane worms. These were supplemented by tinned fish and beef that her elder sister, Mashadi, would send her. My mother refused to get dragged down by what she didn't have, leaning on her father's advice to travel and experience the wonders of the world through reading the many books on his bookshelves and by using her imagination.

A gifted student, Mamphela excelled in all her subjects. In 1964, she moved to Setotolwane High School for her last two years of high school, where she was one of only two girls in her class. Given the dictates of Bantu education, most primary schools for African students did not teach mathematics. Consequently, she first encountered the subject in Form 4 (Grade 11) at Setotolwane.

After her first mathematics class, Mamphela immediately went to the principal, a Mr Scholtz, to confess that she didn't have a clue what she was being taught. Mr Scholtz was open-minded enough to arrange for extra classes for Mamphela and other students who were new to mathematics. On this occasion, the kindness of a teacher helped to level the playing field a little for these young black children. Over the course of the next two years, they covered the entire 12-year curriculum.

By the time she matriculated, my mother had obtained a C for mathematics, a B in biology, an A in physical science and at least a B in all other subjects. Though she passionately wanted to be a scientist, her physical-science teacher, a Mr Gouws, persuaded her to study medicine. A black person, he told her, would never be given the opportunity to rise to the highest level as a scientist and he convinced her that she would be wasting her time if she took that path.

In 1966, when she was just 19, Mamphela Ramphele's first traumatic experience of apartheid exposed her to naked injustice, leaving a lasting impact on her psyche. Kranspoort mission was declared a 'black spot in a white area' and the Ramphele family was forced to leave this fertile land. Until then, the family and their neighbours had lived healthy, comfortable lives. They grew any and every type of crop they desired. The plentiful wildlife provided enough meat to sustain both the villagers and the leopards that roamed the Soutpansberg. Easily accessible aquifers and a decent amount of rainfall also meant that water was plentiful in this part of the country. However, these idyllic conditions attracted the attentions of white farmers, including those whose holdings bordered the mission, who coveted the land. They lobbied the National Party government to move these natives off their land and settle them in a dry, arid region called Indermark, roughly 80 kilometres from Kranspoort.

The Rampheles were allowed to remain for a few more years to wind down the school and to ensure that the teachers, including both my grandparents, were given enough time to find posts elsewhere. It was a particularly difficult time for the Ramphele family since grandfather Pitsi was ill with terminal throat cancer.

My maternal grandfather passed away in May 1967, leaving his family in a vulnerable financial position. Under Bantu education, black teachers at that time had no pension provision regardless of how long they worked; in my grandfather's case, his public service had lasted more than 26 years. As a young widow of 41, with five dependent children, Tsipu had nothing but her meagre monthly salary of R67 as a primary-school teacher to fall back on.

Tsipu finally left Kranspoort mission in 1969 and resettled in Uitkyk at my grandfather's homestead. She secured a teaching job for herself in a primary school in a neighbouring village about ten kilometres away. Taking the traumatic upheaval in their stride, the family enrolled the youngest children in schools and established themselves within the local community.

My grandmother was an excellent teacher, praise singer and disciplinarian, with a wicked sense of humour. Tsipu taught her children self-love, discipline and diligent application to whatever task they were given at home or at school. Whenever I laughed at her boastfulness, she would ask, 'Ngwanaka, if you don't praise yourself, who will do it for you?'

Despite the hardships, her talented and driven children went on to become teachers, a nurse, a mechanical engineering technician-turned-teacher and a junior accounting clerk. Academically speaking, Mamphela was the star of the family. Her academic performance opened doors to her that were shut to many other black people at the time. She started to notice that many white people were willing to help her because they felt she had exceptional talent. This proposition left her with mixed emotions.

Her experience with teachers such as Mr Scholtz was the beginning of a lifelong trend in which my mother would encounter both extraordinary kindness and unconscionable cruelty from white people. For many people of my mother's age, white South Africans who behaved like normal, kind-hearted human beings stood out as memorable exceptions to the majority, who unapologetically enjoyed the benefits of the iniquitous apartheid system.

These tensions between aspirations and reality were not decisions unique to my mother. Charles Sibisi, for instance, had a lifelong dream of becoming an engineer. Even though his school marks were exceptional and should have given him access to any engineering school, this dream was never realised. In a similar way, my father was also constrained by apartheid in his choice of career. He wanted to study law, but his mother, fearing that law would lead him to politics and expose him to harm, advised him to do medicine.

Just one year apart in age, my father and mother grew up as apartheid was seeping into every fibre of society. The Industrial Conciliation Act of 1956 legalised the policy of job reservation, which explicitly forbade black people access to skilled employment in all but a handful of professions. Consequently, my parents were among the first generation of South Africans to fully encounter the effects of this unjust and dehumanising system. The constraints on my parents' career choices were but one of a growing number of daily reminders that the government of their country did not regard black South Africans as human beings of equal value to white South Africans.

That they were unfairly excluded from opportunities their natural talents should have afforded them was obvious. As they stepped out into the world, outside the familiar township or rural cocoon, a previously obscure fact became clearer to both my parents: their families were among a shrinking minority of black families that continued to set high expectations for their children. Through their individual experiences with their peer group, they both began to realise how they had been shielded from the worst effects of apartheid and separate development by the family values that had guided their upbringing. Many black people they encountered were cursed by the burden of low expectations, which I discuss in more detail in Chapter 11. My parents were fortunate in that, despite the material poverty that constrained their upbringing, they did not come from households that had internalised the myth of the inherent inferiority of black people. As my father admitted in the article titled 'We Blacks': 'My friendships, my love, my education, my thinking and every other facet of my life have been carved and shaped within the context of separate development.'[2]

To be sure, separate development meant that the lives of my grandparents, like those of all other black South Africans of the time, were shaped by unequal access to opportunities, unequal pay and the long-term effects of hut taxes, which forced urbanisation and reduced the quality of living for families like the Rampheles and the Bikos. Separate development meant that all black people experienced long commutes, highly demeaning interactions with white people and a constant anxiety about providing for one's family. These circumstances also took a physical toll on my grandparents and later caused them, like many of their age-mates around the country, to suffer from arthritis, hypertension, heart disease and cancer.

In those days, most black people knew that their lives were purposely made miserable by white oppression, but not many of them understood the insidious consequences of accepting the concepts of white supremacy or black inferiority. Thanks to a combination of their upbringing and their intellectual talents, my mother and father had a healthy dose of self-confidence. They learnt from their parents and observed, through their own ability to perform at a high level, that there was no truth to any insinuation of their intellectual inferiority. This gave them a deep self-love to accompany the respect and empathy for human beings taught them by their parents. My parents' generation were confronted with the reality that the apartheid project sought to break the spirit of black people through systematic denigration of their self-worth and self-respect.

This background prompted a keen social awareness that prepared them for the different experiences they were about to have at university.

4

The 'Durban Moment'

My father arrived at the University of Natal in Durban in 1966. He had been accepted by the medical school of what was referred to as the 'University of Natal Non-European section', or UNNE. Like most black students, he had to complete a preliminary year of studies before he could enrol for his first year of medical education.

Steve Biko, like all black students living on campus, was accommodated at the 'non-European residence' named after Dr Alan Taylor, founder of the Durban Medical School. From the start, medical studies was a solid number three on my father's priority list, after student politics and socialising. He quickly made a wide circle of friends, particularly among African and Indian students. By the end of his first year, he had developed a reputation as a charismatic, incisive thinker who knew how to party. Even as they enjoyed themselves at social events, Steve and his fellow students were acutely aware of the disturbing trajectory of the national political situation and the obligation on them as students to do something about it.

Since he was determined to participate in student politics, he promptly joined the only student organisation available to him, the Student Representative Council (SRC). He was soon elected as one of the representatives of the broader University of Natal SRC for the National Union of South African Students (NUSAS). Founded in 1924 by white liberal students led by Leo Marquard, NUSAS attached itself to the twin causes of non-racialism and non-sexism.

In an interview he did more than ten years later, Steve Biko said that when he arrived at the University of Natal, four things could be said about the state of South Africa's political landscape. First, the political crackdown that followed the Sharpeville massacre in 1960, leading to the banning of liberation movements such as the ANC, had inculcated a deep-seated fear among black people. This fear had stopped black people from aspiring to leadership at any level of society. Black people opted to put their heads down and quietly focus on earning a living. As a result, black people started to buy into the idea that they needed to learn their place in society. There was a growing belief that not attracting attention to oneself was the best course of action. This was a natural self-preservation instinct that created a devastating emasculation of black men, and a devaluation of the dignity of black women.

Second, fear among black people created a national leadership vacuum that was filled by young white liberals. Black people no longer felt it was safe to take up leadership roles in organisations that fought for their freedom. Having followed the Rivonia Trial in 1963–1964 and the resultant life sentences received by Mandela and his co-defendants, few black people wanted to suffer the same fate. To my father, the idea of oppression by a white minority being fought by white 'liberation struggle leaders' was unacceptable. He wondered how it could be that white people dominated both sides of the debate. It was clear to him that black people were in all aspects of society only visible in subservient roles. This helped reinforce their sense of inferiority.

Third, my father felt that black people needed to elevate themselves by reconnecting with and reflecting those value systems – ubuntu, self-respect, preservation of fellow citizens' dignity and an ability to speak truth to power – they cherished in dignified, respected people in society. They needed to find a reason to walk tall and look at anyone they encountered as their equal, not their superior. To him, this also meant that, culturally, it was inconceivable that South Africa should look and feel like an island of Europe in Africa. There had to be public celebration of African culture, even if this was done through small acts of rebellion.

Fourth, he observed that true liberation had to start with tackling the fear in the hearts and minds of black people. This could only be done through the demonstration of fearlessness by him and the collective student leadership group he was a part of. He sought to start his journey as a student determined to revive student leadership as a platform for future leadership roles in society. To become the leaders they aspired to be, my father and his colleagues focused, from their first day on campus, on fighting for a decolonised education system.[3]

Based on these four observations, Steve Biko and his fellow student activists opened a new chapter in the country's liberation struggle that has since become known as the 'Durban Moment'. Student leaders demanded that the objective of a non-racial society be dependent on the absence of any form of oppression and saw no logic in distinguishing between different oppressed groups.

This dramatically changed the contours of the battle for equality by breaking down the barriers between Indian, so-called coloured and Cape Malay South Africans. It introduced the word 'black' into the South African lexicon as a descriptor for what were previously called Africans, coloureds, Indians, Bantu or natives. Before then, no other political entity had sought to use the word as a general descriptor for all of South Africa's oppressed people. The idea was that creating such a new identity for the oppressed would counter the perceived superiority of whiteness and allow these young leaders an opportunity to reshape South African identity politics.

It was not a coincidence that my father and his fellow student leaders redefined identity politics in South Africa. From the very beginning, their diverse group defied easy classification. Several Indian leaders were involved in the movement from its infancy. Sathasivan (Saths) Cooper and Strinivasa (Strini) Moodley, both the sons of educators, helped to shape the definition of what the 'black' in Black Consciousness meant. Through plays, music and poetry recitals, Strini and Saths brought an artistic expression of Black Consciousness into the movement.

Two dynamic women, Sumboornam (Sam) Pillay, Strini's wife, and her friend Ashlatha (Asha) Rambally, joined Saths and Strini in the early days of the fledgling movement. They brought their own insights and flair for the performing arts to the table.

Strini Moodley's mother was a housewife and his father was a psychology lecturer. Moodley senior had been politicised through his involvement in the trade-union movement, so Strini grew up in a house where matters of equity and the rights of workers were often the topic of discussion.[4] Travelling on the bus to school, listening to what people were saying, and seeing the harassment of 'people of colour' by the police, he came to the conclusion that South African society was broken by inequality. A big breakthrough came for Strini when he read Frantz Fanon's *The Wretched of the Earth*, which helped him to understand the dehumanising nature of the type of oppression indigenous people had to endure.[5]

Because his mother was of mixed ethnicity, Strini realised there was nothing tying him to a particular Indian identity.[6] He was psychologically prepared to question whether it was best to view himself in ethnic terms or as part of a whole 'oppressed race'. Having undertaken this individual journey, Strini found he had much in common with the rest of the group that met at the Alan Taylor Residence.

Saths Cooper recounts that he was politicised by multiple formative experiences that were rooted in the inequity of apartheid. He grew up on a small farm outside Durban and noticed how his Zulu friends were forced to go to a different school than the one he attended. He told me how his mother, a teacher by profession, decided to set up a small school to teach her son and several children of different ethnicities. Through this act of defiance, Mrs Cooper instilled in her son the will not to meekly accept an unjust situation.

Saths remembers the day he saved a young boy's life as a key turning point in his own politicisation. On his way home from high school, he came to a busy intersection and noticed a group of burly black policemen pummelling a youngster, who looked roughly the same age as him. He went up to the policemen and shouted forcefully at them to stop. One of the senior policemen asked him if he knew the boy, to which Saths responded in the negative. 'I told them that I found it despicable that they would, as black men, enforce pass laws in such a ruthless and mindless way,' he recalled.

The shock of the confrontation with this precocious teenager must have shamed the policemen, as they stopping the beating. Saths Cooper gave the boy a handkerchief to wipe the blood off his face and carried on with his journey.

Uncle Saths arrived at Salisbury Island College, built on the site of a naval base in Durban harbour, unexcited at the prospect of attending an Indians-only school. But he would soon find a more stimulating environment at the Alan Taylor Residence, which was located in Wentworth, on the other side of town. He met Steve Biko in 1968 through intervarsity events and they took an immediate liking to each other. Whenever they were together, their conversation was laced with comedic banter.

As a consequence, Uncle Saths joined a group of roughly 15 people who would meet at the Alan Taylor Residence on weekends to begin a conversation that contributed to the early formulation of what the 'black' in Black Consciousness would be. The expansive idea of who should be regarded as black was not initially understood or endorsed by everyone who would go on to become the founding members of the BCM. Indeed, some teased my father for what they saw as his liberal view of blackness. Klaas Mogotlane, a bright young medical student from Zebediela, in what is now Limpopo province, once comically burst out: 'Biko! No man, you can't die for Indians! Die for us.'

Saths, Strini, Sam and Asha seamlessly integrated into this founding leadership group. According to Uncle Saths, they cemented their ties at the post-meeting 'gumbas' that would always feature music, beers and more conversation. Mixing the social, professional and intellectual elements of their lives strengthened the quality of their relationships and helped to create a family-like environment with a deep sense of trust and love for one another.

There was a growing consensus among these students that the apartheid state had to be opposed by organisations that were led by the oppressed, referred to as 'non-whites' at that time, instead of by white liberals. They were vocal about the distinctions between 'reverse racism' and black pride; for them, the freedom of South Africa could only be won by independent black leadership and not the type of compromised black leaders who ran the Bantustans. They argued that the Bantustan leadership was not an expression of independence, but was instead part of the reactionary machinery of an oppressive system propped up by the tactic of divide and rule. These intellectual positions planted the seeds both for the growth of a black student movement and for the creation of a broader cultural movement that would eventually be called the BCM.

This founding leadership team helped shape the belief that who you identify yourself to be is testament to your inner mental state. The ability to insist on self-definition, and the unwavering desire to create their own identity, was the start of their journey to freedom. This created a sense of 'wokeness' around the BCM ideology that even people who didn't fully grasp the details of the philosophy wanted to be a part of.

Though the positions taken by these students were well thought out and clearly articulated, these high-minded ideas were also grounded in their respective journeys towards self-knowledge. As Marcus Garvey once said: 'Many a man is educated outside the school room. It is something you let out, not completely take in. You are part of it, for it is natural; it is dormant simply because you will not develop it, but God creates every man with it knowingly or unknowingly to him who possesses it, that's the difference. Develop yours and you become as great and full of knowledge as the other fellow without even entering the classroom.'[7]

Black Consciousness sought to awaken the latent greatness within black South Africans from the long slumber that had befallen them under apartheid. All 15 founding members of the BCM had woken from their own personal slumbers many years before they met. They recognised in each other the same thirst to know the answers to a similar set of questions. The group of 15 came together organically, with different members joining in a staggered fashion. Uncle Barney and my mother, for example, were not part of the group at its inception.

Though my mother did not participate in the formative revolutionary conversations taking place at the University of Natal, she was possessed by the idea that something special awaited her in Durban. Her dream had to be deferred, though, because she did not know that she needed to apply early in the previous year to be considered for enrolment into the top universities. Mamphela only applied in September 1966, and was turned down for late application.

After this setback, she was advised by Mr Gouws, her high-school physical-science teacher, to apply to the University of the North for pre-medical courses that would improve her chances of getting into medical school in 1968. In 1967, after completing matric, my mother enrolled at the University of the North, located in Turfloop, just east of Pietersburg (today Polokwane). The students there were mainly focused on social activities rather than political activism. Campus life revolved around lectures and entertainment, including ballroom dancing, sports and picnics.

The trauma of losing her beloved father in 1967, and the financial destitution that overtook her mother, focused Mamphela's attention on making a success of her studies. She applied to the University of Natal medical school, and was accepted for the 1968 academic year. Though her father's death had left her with almost no resources to get to school, let alone money for tuition, my mother was determined to fulfil her dream of obtaining the best available medical training. She borrowed R52 from Koko Ramadimetsa, one of her aunts, to pay for a return second-class train ticket from Johannesburg to Durban. At this point, she had no idea how she was to get money to feed herself or pay her fees.

That she had the chutzpah to show up anyway is revealing of her mental fortitude. When she arrived at the building in Umbilo Road where the medical school was located, Mamphela had to confront the reality that she did not know how she would cover her tuition fees.

Impressed by my mother's tenacity, the school's senior administrator, Mrs Whitbey, let Mamphela know that she qualified for a government loan/bursary scheme that would fully cover her board and tuition. Mrs Whitbey also told her that given her high marks in both matric and her pre-medical courses at the University of the North, she was eligible for two additional scholarships – the Ernest Oppenheimer Memorial Bursary and the South African Jewish Women's Bursary. The extra funds meant that my mother had enough pocket money to allow her to send R20 to R30 home every month – the equivalent of almost half her mother's salary as a teacher.

Mamphela was assigned to the Alan Taylor Residence, a complex of buildings that had served as an army barracks during the Second World War. By pure chance her dorm room was across the passage from that of Vuyelwa Mashalaba, who was a member of the SRC alongside my father. Vuyelwa, who was in her second year, took my mother – a young rural woman with no friends or family in Natal – under her wing. She introduced her to different types of music, notably Miriam Makeba and classical music. Vuyelwa also helped Mamphela pick out more suitable clothes, sewing some of her best dresses herself, and mentoring her in student politics.

Vuyelwa helped my mother to understand how campus life worked and, most importantly, began introducing her to some of the young student leaders on campus. My mother's first exposure to this political environment was when she accompanied Vuyelwa to student assembly meetings called by the SRC at the Alan Taylor Residence. A large group of students gathered to discuss their role in student politics and to receive reports from the SRC. The medical school was part of the UNNE, which attracted some of the brightest black students in the country. My father and Vuyelwa were part of a small group of black students who sat on the SRC at Howard College, on the main campus of the University of Natal, which was strictly reserved for white students.

At the Alan Taylor Residence, Vuyelwa and my mother attended meetings in my father's room, or in rooms belonging to his fellow activists, where the early ideas of Black Consciousness were being discussed. At that time all students at the University of Natal still belonged to NUSAS, whose members were drawn from all 'racial groups'.

My mother recounts how she was transfixed by the mature, articulate nature of this group of students. She was most impressed with how well-read they all were. Her competitive instincts kicked in and she did everything she could to sharpen her own intellectual tools of analysis. She quickly caught up with the literature and jargon used so effortlessly by the more urbane student members to diagnose the plight of the oppressed people of South Africa. By this time my father was a voracious, systematic reader, well versed in the writings of Georg Wilhelm Friedrich Hegel, Marcus Garvey, WEB Du Bois and Frantz Fanon, to name but a few. These works presented both philosophical tools of analysis and case-study material on how people in other countries dealt with oppression in its different forms.

It was largely thanks to Charles Sibisi, by then a classmate of my mother's, that these books were accessible to my father and his friends. Charles, who had started his medical training in 1967, was a quiet, highly intelligent, introspective young man. He played a key role in helping to draft documents, plan and orchestrate alliance structures, and challenge linear thinking. Both his parents were lecturers; his mom, a social anthropologist, taught at Howard College, and his father was a professor of Zulu at the University College of Zululand. Charles's parents had access to the main university libraries, and their international network of colleagues and friends ensured that they could obtain the latest literature by black intellectuals from different parts of the globe. According to Uncle Barney, the US consul-general in Durban also took a liking to these young students and assisted them in sourcing additional reading materials.

An essential question this group of politically active students tussled over was how to articulate their independent priorities as so called non-white students and what organisational format they could use to elect a leadership that could express these priorities in an unapologetic manner. The idea that they needed their own organisation to achieve these goals began to crystallise. Uncle Barney attests to the fact that by 1968, there was no ANC activity in South Africa whatsoever. For all intents and purposes, the banned liberation movement was rudderless and needed a new impetus.

During these early years, the core group of 15 students started to act as a collective and live the values of true non-racialism. The collective consciousness they were developing still lacked a formal structure, but its early manifestations were distinctive. The students sensed that the organisation they would create could be significantly larger in scope than just a student body.

They were all equals, they were meritocratic, everyone's views mattered, they pulled no punches in both their internal and external discussions, they were respectful but direct and robust in the way they argued among themselves. This principled stance shocked outsiders who observed how free they were from apartheid's racial subclassifications of Indian and coloured people, and how clearly and even-handedly they were able to put white racists in their place.

These students realised that they were joined at the hip by a system that viewed all of them as inferior to white people. Despite this understanding, for the next two years they still continued to classify themselves collectively as 'non-whites'. It was only two years later, after they had founded their own student organisation, and had some of their most intense conversations about identity, that they decided henceforth to use the term 'black'.

Naturally, not all 15 students were on the same page about how to move forward. Some of them had a sense of hesitancy in creating an independent organisation. But after they began meeting students from other university campuses, it became clear that students around the country needed an empowering political vehicle that could take the lead in creating a positive identity for marginalised South Africans. Their early interpretations of Black

Consciousness forced them to engage each other intellectually on the trivial nature of ethnic differences. They pushed each other to see just how much they had in common as human beings and how the display of unity among the oppressed would, in and of itself, represent a sign of liberation. Showing the majority of citizens how they could act in unison against apartheid would begin to take apart the divide-and-rule principle at the heart of apartheid legislation.

These students threw themselves into the cause of liberation. During this period, student politics was a 24-hour occupation. It required tireless dedication to the search for the best ideas and constant discussion to advance their budding agenda. Every ounce of their natural talent was directed towards the collective endeavour to ensure that they presented a compelling narrative.

It was during these engagements, in mid-1968, that my parents met for the first time. Though my mother had diligently stuck to her studies and made the necessary adjustments to life far from home in the first half of that year, she was soon sucked into campus political life. From her room across the passage, Mamphela had observed Vuyelwa's busy schedule, which involved her passionate participation in student politics in addition to a full course load as a medical student.

Charles Sibisi told me that there was a high failure rate among black medical students during that period. One reason was that the course work was challenging and the pace of learning was frenetic. The other reason is that there was embedded scepticism on the part of the lecturers (almost all of whom were white) that the black students were capable of the work required. Therefore, the smallest infringement of the rules or sign of underperformance would lead to exclusion.

Vuyelwa Mashalaba, Goolam (Gees) Abram and Steve Biko were the three black student representatives on the SRC. The trio would meet with their fellow black students in the Alan Taylor Residence to canvass their concerns and attend to their key initiatives. These meetings were characterised by robust, intense debates over existential issues related to student politics, but sometimes they were about mundane administrative matters that could make the students' lives a little easier. In these first sessions, my mother was merely an interested observer.

Mamphela Ramphele's presence at these meetings coincided with the first steps taken by my father and his colleagues to form SASO. He was emboldened by the founding in July 1967 of the University Christian Movement (UCM). This was a 'multiracial' and ecumenical body set up by a group of Anglican and Catholic students, together with white liberal students and academics. Barney Pityana was involved in the embryonic stages of the UCM.

Almost as soon as they had the idea for the UCM, Basil Moore, Colin Collins and Motlalepule Winifred Kgware met with Barney to solicit his advice on its formation, and as a result he served on the executive of the organisation. The UCM grew rapidly, setting up 30 branches at seminaries, universities and teacher-training colleges across the country.[8] Uncle Barney and my father had reconnected in 1967, leading to an invitation by Uncle Barney for my father to address a group of like-minded student leaders at the University College of Fort Hare.

In July of that year, the NUSAS national conference was held at Rhodes University, in Grahamstown (today Makhanda). This was a seminal event that laid bare the need for a black-run organisation that would truly represent black students. Despite the lip service paid to unity during the many conference speeches,

Steve Biko (right) and comrades at the funeral of Chief Albert Luthuli, Groutville, 1967.
(Alf Kumalo Family Trust/Africa Media Online)

black students were made to stay at a church building in the local township and had to make their own way to the conference every day, while white attendees stayed close to the conference venue.[9] 'This is perhaps the turning point in the history of black support for NUSAS,' Steve Biko says in *I Write What I Like*. 'So appalling were the conditions that it showed the blacks just how valued they were in the organisation.'[10]

What made this particularly jarring for my father and his fellow black student leaders was that the NUSAS leadership as a collective had caucused prior to leaving for Grahamstown and had agreed that if the black students were asked to use separate facilities, the white students would walk out in protest and in solidarity. Instead of walking out, the white students chose to stay in comfort while their black compatriots were humiliated. This betrayal by the white students at the Grahamstown meeting was the final sign for my father that NUSAS could not be trusted as a vehicle for black student aspirations.

When he set out to return to Durban, my father was still seething from the treatment by his NUSAS colleagues. He decided to stop at the Pityana household in New Brighton. My father and Uncle Barney spent two days deliberating the various mechanics available to them to create a new organisation that would speak to the values, philosophies and goals they both felt so passionate about. They agreed to meet later that year at the next UCM conference, in Stutterheim, where they hoped to canvass these ideas with other black students. Both realised that the conference would be a golden opportunity for a catalytic shift, because it would be the first mass gathering of black students available to them.

Barney Pityana acknowledges that he was slow to embrace the idea of black students deliberately isolating themselves by forming an exclusive political body. Coming as he did from an ANC political tradition that embraced multiracialism, he needed to be convinced of the wisdom of going it alone. Once Biko and Pityana had found common ground on this matter, Barney Pityana lent his network and credibility to the effort to break away from NUSAS.

As a consequence, Biko used the UCM's Stutterheim congress to lead the attending black students to a breakaway caucus. He canvassed the black UCM members to follow through on their dream of creating an organisation that would be truly their own. He emphasised that the agenda of black students could not be successfully set and pursued as long as white students, who had little, if any, grasp of the experiences of black students, were at the heart of the decision-making process.

Steve Biko seized this opportunity to unite the black student leadership and champion the creation of a black student organisation. Not everyone was in favour of this monumental step. The late Ben Ngubane, who was a senior student leader and medical student at the time, was vehemently opposed to leaving NUSAS. Ngubane, an uncle of Charles Sibisi, thought that while the white students might have made a mistake, it would be wrong to alienate them as allies.

My father made the point that while the white students might not have a problem with multiracialism, they didn't have the stomach to oppose racial inequality. He thought that if the white students were not even willing to live with the mild and temporary discomfort that would have come from following their black counterparts to spend the night in a township church in Grahams-town, they would not be able to get their hands dirty or, worse, place their lives on the line when the stakes were higher.

My father would later explain to Donald Woods: 'I realised that for a long time I was holding on to the dogma of non-racism almost like a religion, feeling that it was sacrilegious to question . . . I began feeling like there was a lot lacking in the proponents of the non-racist idea, that much as they were adhering to this impressive idea they were in fact subject to their own experience back at home. They had this problem you know, of superiority, and they tended to take us for granted and wanted us to accept things that were second class.'[11]

As a consequence of the black caucus decision taken at the UCM conference, black SRC members from universities across the country voted overwhelmingly in favour of forming a black student organisation. In December 1968, SASO held its inaugural national conference, where my father was elected as its first president and Charles Sibisi was elected vice president.[12] At this stage, the national conference resolved that SASO would be an independent organisation that was still affiliated to NUSAS.

While these developments were unfolding, my mother moved from interested observer to active participant. In February 1968, Mamphela Ramphele made a conscious decision to become more politically engaged. She felt that one needs to make a choice about what was most important in one's life. She could not find anything more pressing than working towards the freedom of oppressed people. Given her perspective as a relative newcomer to student politics in Natal, she understood how special and talented the founding SASO leadership group was. This convinced her that the group was poised to make a great impact.

As she met with the leadership group more often, she also began to fall in love with my father. At first their relationship was one of mutual yet distant admiration. My father and mother jointly worked on a monthly SASO newsletter. She took down his thoughts, dictated in a stream of consciousness, as handwritten notes. They would discuss the themes at length and agree on changes to sharpen the language. He would then type the first draft, in his somewhat clumsy method of using a single finger on each hand. Often, these newsletters had to undergo further last-minute editing before they were circulated to the largely student audience. These documents later formed the body of I Write What I Like, the book my father became famous for.

From the outset, Mamphela told Steve that she was not available for a romantic relationship because she was in a long-distance relationship with a man she had met in high school. During her time at the University of the North, her relationship with Dick Mmabane, a fellow student, had blossomed and matured.

Mmabane came from a respected black middle-class family, and while he would later drop out of university, his path in life as a businessman was already marked out. But, as many people will attest, the first person you date is not always your first love.

My parents would spend countless hours engaging with the topic for the next newsletter. My mother would sometimes play devil's advocate by taking the opposite line from my father and gradually arguing the issue until they were both satisfied with the conclusion. The similarities in their background and upbringing, and their dedication to reaching truthful conclusions, made these discussions fruitful. Together with the other 13 members of their core group, my parents listened to audio tapes of the Black Power movement in the United States, and they observed how the oratorical skills of the black leaders shaped mass mobilisation in that country. Often fired up by these Black Power speeches, they would sing struggle songs and dance to soul-music records until the early hours of the morning.

The tapes exposed my mother to the ideas of leaders such as Angela Davis and the introduction of feminist politics into the Black Power movement. These views spurred my mother on to do further research on feminist topics. She slowly began to marry these ideas with opposition to racial injustice, and it was from this understanding that she helped craft the feminist approach to the work of the BCM. Mamphela was often accused by other student leaders of dividing the movement by raising feminist issues that SASO leaders felt were not yet a priority. She would reply to these accusations: 'Which part of me is black and which part of me is a woman?'

No one seemed overly eager to take on the loud, defiant, skinny young woman, and so, more often than not, her fellow activists acquiesced. Mamphela's ideas led to a focus on the need for black women to be liberated from their oppression by both white men and black men.

Growing ever closer during this time, my parents were very obviously in love, and eventually both of them realised it was pointless to resist these swelling emotions. They became romantically involved and resolved that my mother would break things off with Dick Mmabane when they next saw each other.

5

A movement is born

By the second half of 1969 the relationship between my parents had blossomed into a full-blown romance, and they become inseparable. In Steve Biko, my mother had met a kindred spirit, someone who was intelligent, witty, hard-working and, importantly for her, politically dedicated to the cause of freedom. She had never met anyone like him. In Mamphela Ramphele, my father had met a fearless woman who was smart, principled, hard-working and fiercely loyal to the cause of liberating black people from oppression.

While they were enjoying the early stage of their relationship, they both looked forward to getting the December holidays over and done with. This would be the first opportunity for Mamphela to end her relationship with Dick Mmabane. Looking ahead, my father decided to write a letter to my mother's family professing his love for her. He wanted to make them understand that he was not an opportunist intent on distracting their daughter from a relationship that they had already blessed.

However, by incredible misfortune, his letter failed to reach its intended recipient. By mistake, my mother had given my father the address of the Mmabanes in Johannesburg, where she would often receive letters ahead of her follow-on train trip northward from Johannesburg. In Johannesburg, Dick Mmabane's family nonchalantly handed him the letter prior to my mother's arrival. After reading the letter, and realising that he was about to be dumped, Mmabane decided to act with haste.

First, Mmabane decided not to give my father's letter to my grandmother, to whom it was addressed, but instead to dispose of it and seek my mother's lifelong commitment. Once Mamphela arrived, before she could say a word, he proposed. Despite her obvious hesitancy, Mmabane pressured her to get married quickly. His mother had passed away in the middle of that year and he presented his marriage proposal as one of his mother's dying wishes. Mmabane explained to Mamphela that he had already put together a delegation, led by his uncles and some elders from my mother's family, that was on its way to her home in Moshubaba, Uitkyk. The negotiations took place in so much haste that my maternal grandmother, Tsipu, was not even able to participate.

The Rampheles, unaware of the new relationship between Mamphela and Steve, were pleased that a well-respected family had come to ask for their daughter's hand in marriage and agreed to the union. Within days, arrangements were made for them to marry. With the hastily arranged wedding behind her, my mother returned to medical school in early 1970 as a married woman. Needless to say, my father was shocked and disappointed. My parents agreed to maintain a working platonic relationship and cut off any romantic interactions between them.

Dashingly handsome, tall, broad-shouldered and usually well-dressed, my father had no shortage of female admirers. He was soon back to his old schedule, working hard and attending parties and socials. Even at this point, he would from time to time try to convince my mother that she had made a mistake that could still be reversed. When it was clear to him that there was no prospect of my mother's changing her mind, he grudgingly decided to move on.

At this point, Vuyelwa Mashalaba introduced him to a relative of hers whom she recommended as a suitable long-term companion. Soon, my father began seeing Nontsikelelo Mashalaba, a beautiful, petite nursing student from Umtata (today Mthatha) who is fondly referred to as Aunt Ntsiki.

These romantic escapades notwithstanding, the first priority on my father's mind was building an organisation that would fill the political void in South Africa. In 1970, during a SASO conference at the Alan Taylor Residence, a decision was made to officially disaffiliate from NUSAS. Uncle Saths remembers that NUSAS also happened to be having their own conference at Eston, in the Natal Midlands, some 75 kilometres from Durban. Saths and Mamphela were asked to hand-deliver the SASO resolution to NUSAS. Midway through the conference, Mamphela triumphantly read the SASO resolution out to the attendees.

In the ensuing discussion, various NUSAS leaders made attempts to convince Saths and Mamphela that they were making a mistake. According to Uncle Saths, they both stuck to their guns, firmly and militantly letting NUSAS know that they were there to inform them of an independent decision, not to seek their consultation. My mother went further still by explaining to NUSAS that black students would no longer participate in the legitimisation of white privilege. She and Saths left without another word, leaving the conference attendees in shock.

In 1969 Uncle Barney was expelled from Fort Hare because of protest action he and his fellow student leaders had launched in opposition to the creation of the segregated university system. At that time, Fort Hare faced the same treatment that had befallen Lovedale, with Afrikaans-speaking lecturers replacing the college's experienced and well-loved faculty. For students who had experienced both Fort Hare and Lovedale at their pinnacle, this drastically changed culture was almost unrecognisable. Rather than validate these changes by continuing to attend university, Pityana and his fellow students decided to protest to the point of being expelled.

At my father's invitation, Uncle Barney moved to Durban and began sharing my father's dormitory room. In his characteristic style, my father arranged for Uncle Barney to eat at the cafeteria, so for all intents and purposes he became a fellow student. Uncle Barney was astounded by the depth of reading achieved by the 14 other founders of SASO. He was already well-versed in the classic literature taught at Fort Hare, but admits to needing to catch up when it came to the wide range of Black Power literature available in and around the Alan Taylor Residence.

During this time Uncle Barney enrolled at the University of South Africa (Unisa) to continue a bachelor's qualification in law. Given that his studies were by correspondence, he was able to fully concentrate on his political work in Durban, becoming secretary-general of SASO.

As time went by, Barney Pityana's wife, Nosidima Pityana (popularly referred to as Dimza) struck up a friendship with Aunt Ntsiki and my father. Both women were nurses, and shared a passion for health care, while Barney and my father were kindred political spirits. This overlap in interests allowed the four to become great friends, and gave Uncle Barney and my father the time and space to work hard to establish the fledgling BCM. Over time, Aunt

Dimza became more involved politically. This made it even easier for Uncle Barney to dedicate himself, knowing that his wife had the necessary context to understand why he needed to spend so much time at work. Uncle Barney explains that as a newly married man, he had no resources to sustain himself and his family, but because the leadership group shared absolutely everything, he managed to make ends meet.

During my father's endless discussions with Uncle Barney, it became clear to both men that the movement they were founding needed to build its political views on solid intellectual ground. These conversations directed their attention to the great European philosophers' arguments for liberty and freedom, leading Biko and Pityana to ask what could be drawn from their conclusions that would resonate with the South African cause. Through this process, they became greatly influenced by the ideas of the German philosopher Hegel, and his understanding of consciousness as a three-layered phenomenon.

According to Hegel, the first layer of consciousness encapsulates the things we sense. The second layer consists of our perceptions of reality and how these perceptions impact the distinction we make between us and the world we live in. The third layer covers our understanding of who we are, distinct from other individuals or groups of people around us.

Uncle Barney explains that while this philosophical approach to consciousness was attractive to them, they wanted to distil a practical political ideology from it that would present a coherent vision to the ordinary South African.

Hegel's third layer of consciousness brought Biko and Pityana back to the idea that black South Africans had to love themselves as individuals in order to break free from the shackles of white people's othering. The breakthrough came with their inclination to take Hegel's conclusions, reached through philosophy (a Greek word meaning 'love of wisdom'), and turn them on their head, seeing a political opportunity to build a movement on the wisdom of self-love.

It was during 1970 that they became intentional in their use of the word 'black' to describe all oppressed people in the country. True to their skill in turning concepts on their head, their sounding-board group at the Alan Taylor Residence morphed the term 'non-white' into an insult to blacks who they felt were kow-towing to the interests of whites. What the Black Power movement in America would call an 'Uncle Tom' became referred to as a 'non-white' within BCM circles. As they began to be more cohesive in their outlook, they understood that defining themselves in the negative, as non-whites, took away their agency and trivialised their majority status in the country. Those who were still trapped in the mindset of being defined in the negative were ridiculed into realising their complicity with the apartheid project.

Taking their cue from Garvey, Du Bois and Fanon, and emboldened by the Black Power movement in the United States, they began expressing themselves as black and proud. A positive self-identity challenged the right of the oppressor to impose himself as the standard by which human beings were to be judged. Having made this critical intellectual breakthrough, this gifted group of young black South Africans was now ready to act on the courage of their convictions.

To them, self-love demanded that blacks as individuals not settle for anything other than what they viewed as best for them as a collective. This political posture made it impossible for Biko and Pityana to accept, much less promote, the idea that black

South Africans should be happy with, for instance, the Bantustans, the racially defined territories set aside by the apartheid government. As Steve Biko once put it: 'Even the whole idea of Bantustans being given freedom – this is a way of accommodating political aspirations of the people which is an inevitable accommodation of what blacks want eventually. But we reject this, what we want is a total accommodation of our interests in the total country, not some portion of it. So we don't have a side programme, we don't have an alternative.'[13]

According to Biko and Pityana, Hegel's three-layered framework offered an explanation for how people had lost a love of self. They believed that black people were ensnared in a vicious cycle of self-doubt that arises from an internalised sense of inadequacy. This sense of inadequacy was drawn from accepting as a fact of life their status as members assigned to a lower rank in society.

Recreating black South Africans' consciousness demanded an overthrow of this basic sense of inadequacy and an end to the reality and perception of inequity. It also demanded an end to the status of black South Africans as second-class citizens. Such demands could only be met through a psychosocial revolution that would make black people fall in love with themselves and each other again. Armed with this analysis, Steve Biko and Barney Pityana espoused five steps towards achieving this psychosocial revolution.

1. **Psychological liberation** through individual affirmation that would lead to a national process where black people's humanity is reasserted. Achieving the goal of reasserting black people's humanity in the national South African political landscape called for the creation of conditions for

consciousness-raising among white people to help rid them of their superiority complex.

My father summed it up as follows: 'All in all the black man has become a shell, a shadow of a man, completely defeated, drowning in his own misery, a slave, an ox bearing the yoke of oppression with sheepish timidity. This is the first truth, bitter as it may seem, that we have to acknowledge before we can start on any programme designed to change the status quo. It becomes more necessary to see the truth as it is if you realise that the only vehicle for change are these people who have lost their personality.

'The first step therefore is to make the black man come to himself; to pump back life into his empty shell; to infuse him with pride and dignity, to remind him of his complicity in the crime of allowing himself to be misused and therefore letting evil reign supreme in the country of his birth. This is what we mean by an inward-looking process. This is the definition of "Black Consciousness".'[14]

2. Creating a **single identity** within the oppressed South African polity that would transcend any effort to subdivide it into meaningless racial categories. According to the BCM, all oppressed people needed liberation from the same oppressive forces, and the chances of attaining liberation were far greater as a unified force. This led to a political definition of blackness, which included those regarded as coloured.

3. Articulating the **quest for meaning** in black people's lives within the context of black theology. According to the BCM, religion had to be reframed in order to transform Christ's

mission from the domineering language of colonial conquest, which viewed the Christian mission as a mission to convert those it defined as non-believers, to the liberating concept of finding Christ within all believers.

Reframing the Christian message in this way required the BCM to champion black theology. The idea was that this would occupy a religious space previously dominated by the Dutch Reformed Church, one of apartheid's chief apologists. They challenged the representation of Christ as a blond-haired, blue-eyed man, which underscored the prevailing racism.

4. There should be **widespread counter-cultural conscienti-sation**, which entailed the celebration of African customs, traditional attire, music and theatre. The BCM supported the resurgence of African-oriented plays, novels, essays, poetry and music. The movement's programmes championed African artistic expression in different forms of cultural protests against oppression, as well as the visual display of acts of rebellion that captured the people's revolutionary spirit. Biko and Pityana always insisted on including the creative expressions of groups such as the Theatre Council of Natal, or TECON, and the musical group Malombo as an integral part of Black Consciousness meetings, not just as add-on cultural items.

5. The **establishment of black community programmes** in townships and rural areas. These programmes were focused on making the ideology of the BCM come to life in the form of tangible efforts to improve the lives of black people in a way that restored their human dignity, self-belief and self-worth, and therefore made them more self-sufficient.

The impetus to enact black community programmes flowed from the Hegelian idea that consciousness was about a personality that both thinks *and* acts. That fit with the African philosophy that responsible adult behaviour is always in support of the common good. SASO members gave of themselves selflessly in such community development, which eventually led to the formation of the Black Community Programmes (BCP), which my father immersed himself in after he left medical school.

While these intellectual ideas were crystallising, the core group of 15 decided to enshrine their beliefs in the form of a living organisational constitution.

The Black Students' Manifesto, made public at the launch of SASO in 1969, articulated many of the core BCM ideas, which were catching fire in student halls, dormitories and cafeterias across the country.

No single person decided that a specific day would mark the launch of the BCM. Instead, the groundswell of agreement around the five principles created an unstoppable cultural tsunami that swept across the country and became the movement. Different students were moved to actualise some or all of these five pillars in communities that needed change. This spontaneous combustion of focused revolutionary fervour made the BCM difficult for the apartheid authorities to detect, understand and make risk assesments of.

The character of the movement mirrored that of its student leaders. It was simultaneously an individual journey of self-realisation through knowledge gathering, reflection and reimagination. It was reinforced by vigorous debates, constant engagement and an intuitive understanding that by following a process from self-hate to self-love, any individual would be catapulted into starting to treat their fellow human beings compassionately and indeed loving them. These twin processes are what led to an immediate transformation in young black students to move from timid, subversive opposition to apartheid towards bold, assertive predispositions against all forms of oppression.

By 1970, my mother was head of the SASO branch at the University of Natal. Her responsibility was to see that each of the five pillars of the BCM found expression in the activities that she and her fellow branch members organised within the region. Like other SASO members, my mother and her colleagues declared themselves black first and students second. This necessitated that they engage black people, who were not students, directly in their communities.

From first-hand experience, they all knew the debilitating nature of poverty. Therefore, they intuitively knew that poverty could not only be tackled by addressing material issues. First and foremost, there had to be a fundamental change in the day-to-day approach to community wellbeing, community education and the aggregation of community social capital.

Saths Cooper recalls how he was blown away by the passion and assertiveness of my mother and Vuyelwa Mashalaba in meetings where they shared their opinions. He believes that their forceful brand of feminist politics was essential to shaking up the patriarchy and ensuring that the BCM didn't start its life as a movement saddled with anti-feminist attitudes.

Mamphela brought this same radical attitude to her community work, stirring women in poor communities to assert themselves in their homes and neighbourhoods. To begin implementing these concepts, the SASO Natal branch worked at a makeshift clinic in a township called Happy Valley. This was a rather neglected enclave in the Wentworth area, south of the Durban city centre, not far from the Alan Taylor Residence. They used their medical and NGO relationships to raise donations for much-needed medical supplies. They found that when black people actively took charge of organising programmes which had clear and well-articulated goals, local and international goodwill could be harnessed to generate the appropriate interventions. Working with local students in the Inanda area north of Durban, they set up another health-care project in which they identified urgent needs in the local community and then came to an agreement with the community on how to address these. Thereafter they would undertake the work needed in collaboration with the community and the Gandhi Memorial Centre at Phoenix, in Durban North.

During 1970 my father and Uncle Barney were invited by the Abe Bailey Institute to present papers at a forum at the University of Cape Town (UCT). Uncle Barney told me how they discussed whether or not to attend the conference, knowing that it was likely to be dominated by white liberals. They eventually agreed to go because they thought it could offer a good opportunity for them to publicly articulate Black Consciousness for the first time.

Uncle Barney wrote his paper by hand. When they arrived at UCT, he asked one of the secretaries to help type it up. Though she was a committed anti-apartheid activist, she was driven to tears by the contents of the paper. 'These are the words of a reverse racist,' she told him.

Indeed, after hearing my father and Uncle Barney speak, the majority of the audience, as well as the journalists who attended, decided that Black Consciousness was a dangerous philosophy. Donald Woods wrote a scathing article denouncing its core message. Even though my father took this reaction as a sign that they had made their mark, he decided to seek out reporters like Woods in an effort to ensure that the public did not misinterpret what Black Consciousness was actually about. In one-on-one sessions, using his enormous powers of persuasion, he won over many journalists, resulting in a more accurate public perception of what the BCM was trying to achieve.

This public-relations effort, combined with the network effect of grassroots student politics, bore fruit in the form of widespread popularity for the BCM and its advocates. As a climax to their 1970 programme of action, a SASO conference was arranged at the Alan Taylor Residence. The guest of honour and keynote speaker was Jakes Gerwel, the anti-apartheid activist and philologist from the University of the Western Cape. This and other conferences were necessary to energise and gather like-minded BCM-influenced people, to share the lessons learnt, to galvanise additional financial support and to reinforce the desired key principles to be implemented in the future.

The December 1970 conference was a success, and everyone, including my mother, left in high spirits. Since the conference took place towards the middle of December, my mother could not go home at the usual time at the end of term. When she finally got back home, she was met by a furious Dick Mmabane, who accused her of not wanting to return to him, and suggested that she might still be involved with Steve Biko.

Mmabane was obviously out of touch with the developments in my father's life. He did not know that my father had genuinely moved on, and that in fact, during the course of 1970, Aunt Ntsiki fell pregnant with my elder brother Nkosinathi, which prompted my father to propose to her. They were married towards the end of that year.

As a result of this unfortunate misunderstanding, Mmabane called a family meeting in which my mother was accused of not being committed to the marriage. Mamphela experienced the pain and frustration of fending off these baseless accusations in front of family members. It became clear to her that here was a man who felt threatened by her independent pursuit of student political activity. Given her unwillingness to sabotage her own career to make him happy, and assuage his own insecurities, Mmabane asked my mother to leave. Over the next few days the two families held many discussions and finally agreed that the two should get divorced.

While she felt a measure of shame and heartbreak for being unfairly cast away by her husband, there was also a sense of relief for my mother. Deep down she knew that Mmabane wasn't the right partner for her and that his personal insecurities would have led to further trouble in the long run. Still, when she returned to Durban in January 1971, she was still very emotional about the divorce and often cried on Vuyelwa's shoulder.

Eventually, she came to accept that she had made a mistake to agree to the marriage in the first place, and that she had to pick herself up and find her own journey forward. My father occasionally checked in on her, but given how much had happened in their lives by this stage, each felt that they would have to live with the consequences of their actions. Uncle Saths confirms that the BCM team that used to meet, especially over weekends, at the Alan Taylor Residence acutely felt the unhappiness that my mother was going through during this period.

Throughout 1971, my mother threw herself into her studies and her duties as an activist, such that by the middle of that year, with her political role in the BCM gaining momentum and her medical studies finally on a firm footing, she was back on top of her game. She looked forward to the day when she could begin practising as a medical doctor, and felt invigorated by the weekly interface with local communities and the often-intense conversations with her colleagues.

By this time, the BCM team had begun to make a profound national impact. They all knew it wouldn't be long before the apartheid government started to understand the scope of their ambitions, and that this would lead to unwanted attention, but for the moment they were finally in a position to reflect on their hard work and celebrate their success.

One day in the second half of 1971, a number of the BCM core team decided to get together for dinner at the home of a BCM supporter in suburban Durban. Both my parents were invited and decided to drive there with other members of the BCM. As they went through the gate and into the house, my father put a handwritten note into my mother's hand. It said something to the effect that 'We owe it to each other to finish the journey that was unceremoniously interrupted by our erratic decision-making'.

After the dinner, my parents returned to my father's room to talk about their relationship for the first time in more than a year. In the past few months both had felt unfulfilled outside their student and political-activist commitments. Though they were not the kind of people who lived comfortably with regrets, they both recognised that their lives were now much more complicated than before, with my mother newly divorced and my father newly married with a child.

While Steve Biko relished the prospect of raising his first-born, Nkosinathi, he was a hopeless romantic who believed that becoming a parent was insufficient reason not to follow the dictates of one's heart. In fact, according to Uncle Barney, my father had talked himself into the position that it was fine to love both of these women so long as he could find a way to be true to himself in terms of how they were treated.

He told my mother that he had never stopped being in love with her. Even though he also loved Ntsiki for the woman she was, he professed a different type of love for my mother. He put his feelings for Mamphela in a poem inspired by John Coltrane's *A Love Supreme*. After discussing their situation and their feelings for each other, they decided that they no longer wanted to be separated, even though both were anxious not to humiliate Aunt Ntsiki.

Shortly after this conversation, the two of them went to tell my father's elder sister what they were thinking, implicitly asking for her blessing. As soon as they walked into the room, Aunt Bukelwa knew that they had rekindled their relationship. Aunt Bukelwa loved my mother and had always wanted my father to be with her because that was when it seemed to her that he was at his happiest. So while she began by reprimanding them for their bad decisions in the past, she gave them her blessing to find a way to put their relationship back together.

Aunt Bandi had the same feeling. In later years she remembered her conviction that the two of them belonged together.

Aunt Bukelwa's blessing was enough to give my parents the courage to face the consequences of their love. They no longer felt inhibited by their past. Instead, they could, for the first time, start to plan for the future.

In late 1971 my parents went on a trip to Johannesburg to meet and consult with BCM leaders in the region. It offered a welcome opportunity for them to spend some quality time together. My mother relates how, on the day of their departure, my father was characteristically late. Consequently, when they got to the railway station they did not have time to buy lunch. To make matters worse, they only had enough money for a return trip in third class, which meant they did not have access to the restaurant carriage.

As anyone who knows my mother can attest, she gets very cranky if she doesn't eat regularly. My father, however, decided to studiously ignore her long face. After they arrived at Park Station, they had to travel by taxi to Alexandra township. By the time they arrived at Bokwe James Mafuna's one-roomed house, they were famished and not in a good mood. Still, even with tempers threatening to flare, my father couldn't resist teasing my mother by asking her in a comic Indian accent, 'Are you hunger, my friend?' This was a private joke that referred to an incident Uncle Barney and my mother had recounted to my father. One day the two of them were sharing a railway compartment with an Indian man who kindly offered them food by repeatedly asking, 'Are you hunger, my friend?' Thankfully, Bokwe Mafuna provided nourishment and the mood shifted to lighthearted banter followed by intense briefings.

Bokwe Mafuna had attended his first SASO conference earlier in 1971 at the Hammanskraal Catholic Seminary. At that time he was a reporter for the *Rand Daily Mail*, but he ended up joining the BCM because he strongly identified with their ideas and plan of action. Mafuna recruited young people such as Welile Nhlapo and Tomeka Mafole as part of a growing cohort of dedicated BCM people stationed in Johannesburg. He wrote many articles and publications shining a light on the work the BCM was doing around the country. Thanks to his efforts, both Steve Biko and the BCM were becoming household names.

The meeting turned into a get-together of BCM people from the Johannesburg area. They all crammed into Mafuna's one-roomed house. These types of gatherings served as outlets, both intellectually and emotionally, to recharge the BCM leadership. The notion that men and women around the country were risking their freedom for a cause that they as leaders were championing gave them the necessary strength to make the public case for Black Consciousness as a new way of life necessary to mobilise black people to liberate themselves from the oppressive racist system.

Upon their return to campus, the whispers about the newly rekindled relationship spread through their circle of friends. One day Vuyelwa Mashalaba confronted my father about his cheating on her cousin. She was livid, and did not accept my father's explanations for why he was knowingly breaking Aunt Ntsiki's heart. Sadly, this cost both my father and mother their relationship with their once dear friend, Vuyelwa.

Aunt Ntsiki had obviously also been informed about my parents' getting back together. A part of her must have known that her husband had loved Mamphela long before she had met him, but still she was determined to fight for her marriage. After all, they also shared a special bond that had been enriched through the birth of their son. This set the stage for a three-way entanglement between three strong-willed young adults. This entanglement would last several more years before coming to a tragic conclusion.

6

Faith and faithlessness

Saths Cooper remembers 1972 as a pivotal year, with strike action led by the BCM taking place on several campuses around the country. Biko had just returned from Hammanskraal, where he had attended a SASO conference where Jerry Modisane was elected as its leader. This came after Themba Sono had resigned as SASO president and was expelled from the organisation for asking the conference to reconsider the policy of non-collaboration with the Bantustans. The strikes resulted from the expulsion of Abram Onkgopotse Tiro following his address at the University of the North's Turfloop campus where he criticised the inhumane standards of the residences, the bad food in the cafeterias and the humiliating treatment experienced by black students.

SASO members asked Steve Biko to personally lead a nationwide strike in support of the Turfloop students, with the objective of changing the conditions there. At Uncle Saths's insistence, they first called for national solidarity on the matter at the newly created University of Durban-Westville (now part of the University of KwaZulu-Natal), which catered for a predominantly Indian student body that was known for being conservative. One of the students, Pravin Gordhan, had been at high school with Uncle Saths. Pravin

Abram Onkgopotse Tiro, circa 1972.
(Ronnie Kweyi/Times Media Group/Africa Media Online)

and others took the view that mass action in the form of a strike would be counterproductive because they were about to write exams, and this would cause great harm to many students who could not afford to repeat a year.

As this view attracted increasing support, Uncle Saths took to the stage and made an impassioned plea for strike action in solidarity with fellow black students. 'I used all the Mahatma Gandhi quotes I could remember,' he told me. His appeal to the better nature of these more conservative students won the day, and set off a domino effect that saw universities joining one after the other. It led to a successful mass-action campaign in May 1972 that demonstrated the national popularity of the BCM and its ability to positively effect change.

Steve Biko addressing a SASO conference, 1972.
(Alf Kumalo Family Trust/Africa Media Online)

However, the BCM leadership group was hardly able to enjoy
the moment. In December of that year came news of the death
of Mthuli ka Shezi, a 25-year-old playwright and political activist
whom my parents had got to know when he was a student at the
University of Zululand. He had risen in the ranks of the BCM until
1972, when he was elected vice president of the Black People's
Convention (BPC). His writing emphasised African identity,

culture and spirituality, and many of his plays were strongly influenced by the ideas of Biko and Frantz Fanon.

Shezi had come to the defence of an African woman who was being drenched with water by a white station cleaner at the main railway station in Germiston. He was pushed in front of a moving train and later died from his injuries. Today, he is known as a symbol of the struggle of black South Africans against the apartheid government, and in 2003 was posthumously awarded the Order of Luthuli in silver. In 1972 he was just another addition to a growing pile of dead black bodies used as cannon fodder by insecure white racists who endeavoured to show their strength. South Africa was beginning to become numb to the loss of black life. Shezi's youth, and his proximity to the other BCM leaders, jolted the movement and hardened its members' resolve to ensure that he had not died in vain.

The murder of Mthuli ka Shezi brought death to the doorstep of the BCM for the first time. Previously, the BCM leaders had considered death a remote possibility but not an inevitable outcome of the intellectual arguments they were making. Suddenly, with Shezi gone, they realised that death could overtake any of them. There is something about close brushes with mortality that obliges any human being to deal with existential questions. As young adults in their early to mid-twenties, they had to reconcile themselves both to the possibly terminal consequences of striving for the cause of freedom and to how their maker would judge their actions.

Those who knew Steve Biko attest to the fact that he was never scared of death. As his friends and co-workers were arrested and killed, he began to understand that dying for a cause was just as important as living according to a set of principles. Biko agreed with Marcus Garvey's view: 'Fear is a state of nervousness fit for children and not men. When man fears a creature like himself, he offends God, in whose image and likeness he is created. Man being created equal fears not man but God. To fear is to lose control of one's nerves; one's will, to flutter, like a dying fowl, losing consciousness yet alive.'[15]

As arrests became more frequent, Uncle Saths recalls that the group took a more confrontational approach in their interactions with the police, demanding that officers justify themselves and prove their bona fides, and insisting that the police address them in English. This posture let the police know that they were not feared and had to deal professionally with the BCM leadership or face the appropriate legal or physical consequences.

As violence and the threat of death hung over the group of 15 young leaders and their growing support base, a spiritual dimension to the socio-political arsenal they had amassed seemed called for. Though the group came from diverse backgrounds, most of the BCM leaders had had a Christian upbringing, which prompted them to consider what appropriate spiritual element should be introduced into their political programme. They felt it was important that the group find healthy spiritual outlets that would strengthen their resolve to continue on an increasingly dangerous political path.

Because different religions and different Christian denominations were represented within the BCM, the group took a liberal approach to religious observances. At the Alan Taylor Residence, the residence committee would host religious leaders from various backgrounds to conduct Sunday services. At the time, the leaders of the BCM were sceptical of the value of established religious practices given that their analysis made them understand the dangerous role Christian missionaries had played in enabling the colonial enterprise and undermining respect for their indigenous culture.

My mother remembers how a small group of activists once attended a service conducted by the Reverend Ernest Baartman, a Methodist. While Reverend Baartman gave a rather long but engaging sermon, my parents unconsciously showed their scepticism by smoking during the service. When the service was over, Reverend Baartman sought out the two offending young people, curious to engage them about their smoking. Seeing the minister come towards them, my father thought they had angered him, and in his typical self-deprecating way made light of the incident.

As the three talked, they got a deeper sense of one another and the Reverend Baartman began to better understand what the Black Consciousness philosophy was all about. This would be the beginning of a long friendship. Eventually, Reverend Baartman was so inspired by the teachings of the BCM that he became one of the first religious figures to declare that the church could not remain neutral in its teaching while apartheid waged a war on good, morally upright black people. He was candid in declaring that the alienation of black people from land that was rightfully theirs was the symbol of all the other assaults on black people's dignity. His theological militancy would earn him the title 'The Black Moses'.

Initially, Uncle Barney was wary of SASO and the BCM becoming a vector for an alternative Christian message. Even though he was a devout Christian who belonged to the Anglican Church, he thought this could narrow the organisation they were trying to build. To his surprise, both the UCM and the Catholic Priests' Association actually approached SASO to ask it to help them think through how to frame a new Christian message.

Both Pityana and Malusi Mpumlwana, another important member of the leadership group, came from strong church-based families and retained a deep Christian faith throughout their time in the BCM. They were part of a significant contingent of BCM leaders who brought strong belief systems and religious ties that connected the BCM with many black theologians. These deep connections between various church traditions and the BCM were facilitated by a shared political agenda, a commitment to honest, transparent interactions, and a set of common life experiences that were conducive to the forging of intimate, long-lasting friendships between members of faith-based communities.

Steve Biko's friendship with Malusi Mpumlwana played an important role in opening his eyes to how faith and African spiritual systems could be married. Mpumlwana had arrived in Durban to study medicine at the University of Natal in January 1971. However, when he met my father and his BCM colleagues, he lost interest in his studies and decided to immerse himself in the activities of the movement.

Born and bred in a rural village just outside Umtata, Uncle Malusi was the grandson of Reverend Michael Mpumlwana, one of the founders of the Order of Ethiopia (iBandla lamaTopiya), an African religious group that broke away from the Wesleyan Methodist Church in 1896. African theologians such as Mata Dwane, Michael Mpumlwana, Marcus Gabashane, John James Xaba, Mangena Maake Mokone and others worked through the Anglican Church to establish the Order of Ethiopia. Mata Dwane was made the first deacon in 1900 and was ordained as a priest in 1911.

The urge to break away and form an independent church was long in the making. Missionary boarding schools set up in the then

Cape Colony during the late 19th century encouraged the blossoming of a modern African nationalism. Some of the missionary boarding-school graduates became priests. Over time, they began to complain about the treatment of black people in the church, and especially the discrimination in terms of salaries, the lack of equal opportunities and the paternalism and overt racism.

Mata Dwane's grandson Sigqibo was born in 1941 and, as was his destiny, became the first bishop of the Ethiopian Episcopal Church. Sigqibo Dwane and Malusi Mpumlwana were close friends and both established a relationship with my father. That their grandfathers had been integral to the formation of the Ethiopian Church was key in establishing a relationship between the BCM and the many talented black priests of the Order of Ethiopia. Sigqibo Dwane became part of growing group of black theologians who would support the BCM in its opposition to Christianity being used to support white supremacy.

Sigqibo did not become a bishop through nepotism. A deeply theological man from early in life, he had studied up to PhD level and was a talented preacher. In his doctoral thesis, Sigqibo analysed the relationship between the Order of Ethiopia and Xhosa spirituality. He wrote that it would be a mistake 'to treat Xhosa religion as a tottering institution which, if left alone, will soon come to its inevitable end. The church has got to raise the question whether this tradition is or is not compatible with the Gospel. The position taken in this thesis is that there is here a challenge to the church in that part of the world, to "de-hellenize" and "de-westernize" itself so that Christ of the new covenant community can manifest Himself to the Xhosa people as "Umntu wegazi lethu" (our real brother), and "umntwana wegazi" (family).'[16] In their intimate conversations on these matters, Uncle Malusi would echo these sentiments to my father. Steve Biko was deeply moved by these ideas.

His mother, Mamcete, regularly attended church services in Ginsberg township and had raised him and the rest of her children as God-fearing, church-going Christians. Though my father finished his secondary education at a Catholic school and was influenced by the Catholic nuns who were his teachers, he remained loyal to the Anglican Church. He occasionally attended services with my mother, introducing her to the Anglican tradition, which she fell in love with, and as a consequence adopted as her own.

Even though he was brought up in the Anglican tradition, he never felt intellectually at ease in the church as an African Christian struggle fighter. These different aspects of his identity clashed with each other, and he wrestled with this conundrum for many years before he found a way to reconcile them.

As a young man, my father had questioned the symbols of European faces in the church, the themes of European history in church hymns and the meaning of the Christian message as it pertained to black people. The Catholic nuns at Mariannhill had encouraged his theological inquiry, and never grew impatient when he challenged them about the theological validity of the Holy Trinity, the ethnicity of the historical Christ and how the church had condoned the treatment of black people.

As a student in Durban, Biko debated with various people about these issues until he found a cogent articulation of what the BCM could do to help transform the South African faith-based community. According to Barney Pityana, though Steve Biko was not overtly religious, he saw an opportunity to use those who preached from the pulpits as political change agents.

In 1972, Steve Biko, then 26 years old, decided to address a conference of black clergymen. He began his address by stating,

'To my mind, religion can be defined as an attempt by man to relate to a supreme being or force, to which he ascribes all creation.'

Though this sentence may seem innocuous, it strikes me as profound that even back then my father knew that Africans do not naturally, as is the case in the European Christian tradition, personify God. Even at that young age, Biko understood that God was an all-encompassing life-force that permeated every aspect of African life. As a liberation philosopher, Biko had no choice but to challenge the prevailing understanding of scripture and the role of the clergy in comforting and stimulating black congregations.

Biko went on to describe the three common characteristics of all religions, namely, that they form man's moral consciousness, attempt to explain the origin and destiny of man, and lay claim to the definitive truth about the nature of the supreme force and what it hopes for humankind.

This was also the basis for his four criticisms of the church. First, the church encouraged black people to turn the other cheek instead of confronting oppression. Second, it was stunted by bureaucracy. Third, it made itself the unquestioning custodian of white values. Finally, an enduring challenge faced by the church was that its impact in the community was limited by its narrow theological approach.

As a solution to the dire picture Biko painted about the church and its future in a radicalised black South Africa, he suggested the introduction of black theology. He described black theology as a situational interpretation of Christianity that seeks to relate black people's present reality, as oppressed partial citizens of their own country, to God. In my father's view, black theology was necessary to shift the moral responsibility to comply with laws that were sinful and corrupt away from black members of the congregation.

Instead, black theology places the responsibility on white people to confront their anti-Christian actions, repent and begin an internal transformation process that can help them become whole South Africans. According to my mother, BCM members were amazed at my father's eloquence and bravery when discussing such important spiritual issues with men of the cloth, who were in most cases much older than him.

It took an acute mind to see through the widespread Christian propaganda and call out its effect on black communities. The church at the time loomed large as an unchallengeable authoritative institution. Both my parents' families were compliant members of church congregations, hence it must have been a shock for them to see the extent of my father's willingness to challenge this existing order. My mother's family was religiously conservative, a disposition likely influenced by both my maternal great-grandparents' profession as evangelists. Her family held on to a tradition of loyal membership of the Dutch Reformed Church. My grandmother never willingly missed a service and she made sure all her children participated in church activities. Throughout his life my maternal grandfather was an active church elder, an interpreter for the Afrikaner dominee (minister), and the local church choir conductor. My grandmother was a proud choir member who had a beautiful soprano voice. Praise and worship were a part of family life that the Ramphele clan cherished and honoured in that unquestioning way many rural black families have learnt to do.

The history of the Dutch Reformed Church is tied to the establishment of a settlement at the Cape of Good Hope in 1652. For the first 150 years both white settlers and black converts were members of the church in equal standing. It was not until 1859 that separate congregations for black members became the norm. After 1881, Dutch Reformed churches, such as the one attended by the Ramphele clan, littered the countryside and urban townships. Each congregation became highly segregated, matching the colour coding that was becoming a central element of South African life.

As membership of the church became increasingly politicised, so too did scriptural interpretation. The message my mother would have heard in church during the 1960s and 1970s, for example, featured an interpretation of a creation story that did not end with Adam and Eve's expulsion from the Garden of Eden. The story of creation, according to orthodox members of the Dutch Reformed Church, continued through the story of Noah to the eleventh chapter of the Book of Genesis, where the people of the Earth, having a single language, decide to build the Tower of Babel to reach up to heaven. Preachers emphasised that this act caused God to fulfil his covenant with Noah and create different languages and 'scattered them abroad over the face of the earth'.

This story was essential to the laying of the theological groundwork for the policy of apartheid and its claim to separate development. This teaching made the congregation aware that God had his favourite people in different parts of the world. Scripture was taught in such a way as to leave no doubt who God's chosen people were in South Africa. It was taken for granted that being dutiful, respectful and deferential to God's people (whites) would enable black people to be regarded with favour on Judgment Day.

It is small wonder, then, that my mother rejected this message and turned to what she felt was a denomination that was less overtly racist. Given her exposure to theological chauvinism, she strongly supported the BCM's push to establish black theology in South Africa. In the search for an appropriate black theological expression, my father's attention was drawn to a new type of Christian message propagated by the Black Power movement in the United States. Intrigued by these ideas, he soon discovered a book titled *Black Theology and Black Power* by James Cone. I'm sure my father would gladly have admitted that he owed many of his insights about the church and its potential role in South Africa's liberation to Cone, who was roughly ten years his senior.

James Cone was born in 1936 in Fordyce, Arkansas, a town that at the time of his birth had 1 200 residents, 400 of whom were black. As a child, Cone asked his father why he preferred the uncertainty of self-employment to that of a steady job in the local sawmill. To this, Cone senior responded: 'My son, a black man, cannot be a *man* and also work for white people.'

Like many African Americans, Cone grew up in a church-rooted family, and as a consequence adored the writings, speeches and teachings of Martin Luther King, Jnr. As he developed intellectually and became a distinguished theologian in his own right, Cone began to question King's accommodationist ideas. He joined a contemporary debate taking place across America about what the appropriate response by black people should be to nationwide acts of oppression and subjugation. For James Cone, these debates revolved around finding God's role in black people's emancipation.

Biko agreed with Cone that black theology starts by asking what the relationship is between black oppression and the Christian gospel. In answering this question, Cone would say: 'There was a need to emancipate the gospel of its whiteness so that blacks may be capable of an honest self-affirmation through Jesus . . . If the gospel is a gospel of liberation for the oppressed, then Jesus is where the oppressed are and continues his work of liberation there.'[17]

Inspired by this view, Biko insisted that it was essential to contest the narrative that God somehow favoured other ethnic groups over black people. This breakthrough would be the first step in freeing black people from the guilt carried by the misinterpretation of scripture condemning them as descendants of the cursed Ham. My father was not the only South African who was influenced by Cone's ideas. Uncle Barney remembers being astounded by the transformation of Methodist theologian Basil Moore when he returned from the US and wrote a seminal paper titled 'Black Theology in South Africa'. The radicalisation of white theologians such as Moore made Uncle Barney recognise the hunger of some clergymen for a message that better spoke to the moment in which they preached.

The next step was to find a way to reverse the tendency of preachers to choose verses from the Bible that alienated the black congregation. My father used the concept of spiritual poverty to describe this tension between black people's lived reality and what they were asked to believe in church: 'The first result of spiritual poverty is that people are distracted from issues that affect their communities; in other words, the gospel becomes irrelevant to pressing communal issues of the time.

'The second result is that black people read the Bible with a gullibility that is shocking. The reaction of the young generation to this gullibility is to drop the church altogether, because they cannot understand the "well-meaning God" who allows people to suffer continuously under an obviously immoral system.'[18]

The challenge Biko laid at the door of black clergy was to find a message that spoke to the contemporary struggles of black people and to their aspirations for a better life for their families. To be effective proponents of black theology, pastors had to dig deeper into their theological understanding to bring biblical lessons that people could relate to. Pastors had to stop speaking down to people and share with their congregations the many ways in which the Bible championed truth, righteousness and restorative justice.

The debates happening in South Africa had occurred a decade earlier in the United States. As people like Cone had tried to define a Christian's duty to withstand oppression without retaliation, black clergymen in the US had been challenged to find a message that was morally responsible and politically acceptable. Though people from different walks of life were contributing different ideas to the Black Power movement in the late 1960s, the central debate was between those who embraced King's charge to love thine enemy, on the one hand, and those who were attracted to Malcolm X's belief that white people were the devil incarnate who should be repelled by any means necessary, on the other.

King put forward the following view: 'How do you go about loving your enemies? I think the first thing is this: In order to love your enemies, you must begin by analysing self. And I'm sure that seems strange to you, that I start out telling you this morning that you love your enemies by beginning with a look at self . . . A second thing that an individual must do in seeking to love his enemy is to discover the element of good in his enemy . . . Agape is something of the understanding, creative, redemptive goodwill for all men. It is a love that seeks nothing in return. It is an overflowing love; it's what theologians would call the love of God working in the lives of men.'[19]

My parents and their fellow BCM leaders recognised the form of love King was describing – agape – as akin to how ubuntu charges Africans to love. But within both the Black Power movement and the BCM, the question was asked whether this was the best form of love for oppressed people to have towards a declared enemy.

Malcolm X answered this question with an emphatic 'no'. In 1963, at a speech he gave at the University of California at Berkeley, Malcolm X argued for a less accommodating approach to racist whites: 'The Honorable Elijah Muhammad teaches us that our people are scientifically maneuvered by the white man into a life of poverty . . . That old Uncle Tom-type Negro is dead. Our people have no more fear of anyone, no more fear of anything. We are not afraid to go to jail. We are not afraid to give our very life itself. And we're not afraid to take the lives of those who try to take our lives. We believe in a fair exchange.'[20]

Malcolm X was joined in his militant stance by Stokely Carmichael, an important Black Power and Black Panther leader who was popular in South Africa because of his marriage to the superstar singer Mariam Makeba. According to Charles Sibisi, the BCM contingent was moved by the following statement by Carmichael: '[I]t is clear to me that we have to wage a psychological battle on the right for black people to define their own terms, define themselves as they see fit, and organise themselves as they see it.'[21]

Through these emotional and intellectual connections to the Black Power movement in the US, the debate found its way into the South African discourse in the 1970s, forcing BCM leaders to argue about the morality of the use of violence against apartheid operatives and whether or not the use of terror as a weapon against white citizens was ever justifiable as a means to a just end.

As always, Biko argued that as a cultural movement, the BCM should retain the moral high ground. For my father, freedom and reconciliation were symbiotic goals that had to be achieved in the right way.

He explicitly agreed with Cone's view that the gospel requires that all captives should be set free, because all people are created and sustained by God. No one can be free until all are free. Cone maintained that reconciliation is a Christian requirement, but he also said that as long as white Christians participate in the oppression of blacks and other groups, reconciliation cannot occur on white terms. This view was adopted by Biko and the BCM leadership team. Although most of them had been beneficiaries of Christian missionary education, they had a long-held suspicion that missionaries could not be trusted as loyal, long-term political allies.

The suspicion of Christian missionaries was well warranted. Ever since Christian missionaries started converting Africans to Christianity, their condoning first of slavery, then of a system of unjust taxation and eventually the system of apartheid, had left them with no credibility within the black freedom-fighting community. Missionaries were believed to have always been in cahoots with white imperial interests, and as such they could not be viewed as trustworthy partners of the movement to liberate black people.

Furthermore, missionaries laughed at and demonised the God concept of black South Africans. By labelling all Africans as pagans who worshipped idols, bowed to superstition and loved many gods, missionaries succeeded in trivialising and vilifying African Traditional Religion. There is no greater form of destruction of the cultural foundations of a people than to succeed in getting them to repudiate their God. It affects every part of their belief system and world view. The result is severe psychological trauma, which some people might find difficult to understand.

All moral judgements are made with an underlying belief system that is weighted in the direction of what we think our creator smiles or frowns upon. To restore the moral foundation that is critical to black self-love, the BCM had to remarry black people's traditional African belief systems with their Christian God concept. This gargantuan task was given to black theology.

Another important task of black theology was to try and restore the faith of the many black people who had given up religion and become atheists. The cruelty of apartheid and its many petty laws, which were designed to humiliate, trivialise and devalue black families, led some black people to turn away from God. As the American novelist and activist James Baldwin once wrote so eloquently, 'no matter how often whites went to church, no matter how often and adamant their claims to be Christians, Christians simply did not act the way whites acted . . . '[22]

It is no coincidence that the 1960s and 1970s were a time of rapid growth in the number of people who identified as communist. Atheism became an obvious position to take for those who could no longer trust in the essential goodness of humankind to self-correct, nor trust in the essential fairness of God to right wrongs.

Members of different liberation groups could identify with Marx's famous quote that religion was the opiate of the masses. The mark of intellectual capability was not to defend what was viewed as the indefensible (Christianity or any other religion), but instead to assume the role of the religious cynic. Non-believers would mock their compatriots for their continued faith in what communists sometimes jokingly referred to as 'an imaginary friend'.

My father, however, did not yield to this peer pressure. He was resolute in his belief in a higher power. In a paper he delivered at the Abe Bailey Conference in 1971, Barney Pityana famously said: 'Black man, you are on your own.' This echoed my father's belief that the combination of apartheid laws and the state-driven capitalism pursued by the National Party had left black people on the periphery of the socio-economic system. While he disdained capitalism and what it was doing in the black community, Steve Biko's belief in the concept of self-determination did not allow him to support an economic system such as communism that depended on central planning. His economic solution for South Africa was undergirded by people-centred socialist policies. Socialism was attractive because it allowed individual self-expression while distributing economic gains to the poorest in society.

To add insult to injury, when black people went to church on Sunday, their church told them they were cursed to remain in this peripheral role for life. Biko believed a key step to liberation was to break the hold this spiritual curse had on black South Africans.

In his support of black theology, my father did not yield to the need to separate Christianity from traditional African spirituality. He understood that for black people, spirituality was a way of life. Black theology blended Christianity and traditional African spirituality to create a syncretic form of faith that became black people's lifeblood. As oppressed people, they saw Christianity differently from the oppressor. Black theology would allow them to read the Bible as a book that supports the underdog. My father felt the biblical term 'Son of man' (often repeated by Stanley Ntwasa, a leader of the UCM) reminded people that the life of Christ was based on a fight against forces that held his fellow men and women captive.

One black theologian who took his cue from Steve Biko was Simon Maimela. After receiving his BA from Unisa, Maimela went on to get a PhD in theology from Harvard University. He used his expertise as a contextual theologian to ask follow-up questions to the ones raised by Biko. Maimela argued that all Christians needed to be reminded that salvation is a gift that God alone can give, because God accepts all sinners unconditionally in and for the sake of Christ. For Maimela, the church needed to return to the Lutheran idea that faith alone should justify a sinner's receiving God's grace.

This dovetailed well with Biko's call that black theology should 'shift emphasis from petty sins to major sins in society, thereby ceasing to teach people to suffer peacefully'.[23] Knowing that those who fought for freedom on Christian principles were operating with the grace of God gave liberation activists the additional impetus needed to see their cause through to its logical conclusion.

The type of black theology that my father supported was oriented towards black South Africans who felt most downtrodden and oppressed by the system. They needed a message of hope that would give them fuel to keep fighting for freedom. Preachers who espoused this message took up the charge in townships and rural areas around the country. They would teach that God's righteousness was especially reserved for those who had little or nothing in this world. Congregations were made to believe that their independence from worldly things was the ultimate liberation. They were free from the mental chains that normally delude people into thinking that possessions and material wealth can provide security and freedom from anxiety. This true sense of freedom would stand them in good stead when building a lasting relationship with God.

This is not to say that black theology pacified people to submit to poverty. On the contrary, the call was to become indifferent to one's material state so that one could focus on the more important spiritual task of self-mastery. Once one completed this journey, the natural next step was to demand the creation of an equitable society.

These black theologians called for liberation within the individual spirit of members of the congregation and solidarity in the fight against injustice as the preconditions for the political freedom they prayed that God would help deliver. They supported the BCM's call for blacks to release themselves from the mental slavery of believing the lie of black inferiority. They viewed this charge as a precondition for individuals to become more effective champions of political freedom.

The founders of the BCM believed that freedom is an indivisible phenomenon. They needed to love themselves and reject the lie of black inferiority in order to free themselves from the bondage of oppression. To love themselves, they had to reaffirm the belief that they too were special in the eyes of their creator. This internal peace gave them the space to believe that this process can and must be reciprocated by white people. Once whites rejected the lie of white superiority, they too would be free from the bondage of oppression.

Steve Biko believed that only by embracing black people's passionate participation in the reshaping of the country could South Africa as a whole enjoy the fruits of re-humanisation. In her current role as founder of ReimagineSA, my mother often makes the point that modern South Africans have only gone halfway on this journey. She believes that while most indigenous people have forgiven white people, the majority of whites have failed to honestly account for what they have done, hence they are not in a position to forgive themselves. As a result, South Africans are wounded by multiple centuries of physical, emotional and spiritual abuse. The cycle of woundedness will not stop without white people's genuine contrition for the benefits they derived from a system that wounded, and continues to wound, their compatriots.

According to black theology, the first step to healing is to accept that these are wounds carried by humans who have the same maker. Because this maker is everyone's God, not just the God of white people, we have to accept that the welfare of all humans carries equal status in the eyes of the divinity. Thus, we remain haunted by the daunting task of making our nation compliant to our cumulative duty of atonement. It is not an option to do nothing because the task is seen as too big or intimidating.

7

Harnessing the power of ubuntu

In May 1972, 15 of the BCM's top leaders from across the country went through a leadership training programme run by Anne Hope. At the time, Anne was also running workshops called 'White on White' that were based on her understanding that racism was essentially a white problem. The central idea behind 'White on White' was that white people were the ones who needed to learn to process and help make sense of the concept of different but equal.

Anne had grown up in an upper-middle-class home in Johannesburg and had a master's degree in education from Oxford University. While studying in the United States, she had been exposed to the work of Paulo Freire, the influential Brazilian educator and philosopher. She grew to love and teach Freire's methodology of conscientisation, elaborated in his most famous work, *Pedagogy of the Oppressed*. Based on her upbringing and insights gained throughout her years as an educator, Anne believed she was in a unique position to help conscientise white people in South Africa about the pathology of racism.

After hearing about her workshops, and understanding that her work was codifying a significant aspect of what he intended the BCM to be about, Steve Biko asked Anne to work with the BCM leadership team, focusing on literacy for liberation.

Anne was a gentle, playful but regal-looking woman who had a deep love for Africa. She was an odd combination of an idealist with a pragmatic sense of how to bridge the gap between theory and practice. She was also openly lesbian, which in the 1970s put her in a unique position to understand how it felt to be discriminated against.

Most of all, Anne had a deep-seated belief in the principle of fairness. She knew how unjust it was that someone of her background had been able to go to Oxford, by virtue of what the English saw as 'pedigree', while the many smart black students she had met throughout her life were shamelessly denied the opportunities they deserved. She thought it senseless for a relatively wealthy country such as South Africa to have so much poverty. Anne was also part of the Grail Community, a Catholic religious group that sought to harness Christian values for positive social change.

Anne strongly identified with Freire's ideas and how he reinserted people into liberation politics. During the 1960s and 1970s, Marxism, with its strong emphasis on class warfare and the need for the working class to control the means of production, had made many of its proponents mechanise the political economy, and in the process they forgot that people were at the heart of the systemic oppression analysed by Karl Marx. Freire found a way to balance class analysis with a psychosocial analytical framework. He believed, for instance, that the fear of freedom felt by many oppressed people is reflected in their attitude to change. His research confirmed that this fear of freedom sometimes compels people to subconsciously choose policies that uphold the status quo.[24]

Ultimately, Freire's philosophy rested on valuing education as a tool to free the minds of oppressed people from the fear of freedom. Once they overcome this fear, they are enabled to learn how to free themselves. He felt that a key job of a liberator is to awaken what he called the 'selfhood' that lay dormant within the majority of oppressed people.[25] According to Freire, enlivening this selfhood is the first step towards helping oppressed people overcome the culture of silence. Once people are liberated to say what they need and want, and what they will and will not accept, then they can use this articulation of their lived reality to begin designing solutions that will address their problems appropriately.[26]

These ideas had a profound effect on the development of the BCM's philosophy. The workshops would help frame Biko's approach to white people, distilling in his mind what their role in South Africa's liberation could be. It was from Freire's ideas, and some of Hope's workshop material, that my father began to understand that white people were projecting a superiority complex that seemed to be their justification for their role as oppressors.

Upon closer consideration, it became clear to Biko that, paradoxically, this superiority complex had its foundations in insecurity. Many white South Africans do not know who they are without reference to their skin colour and how it differs from the indigenous people of the country. Their need to rank, order and subdivide human beings is as much an instrument of privilege preservation as it is their identity. In light of this, Biko understood that white people themselves needed to be liberated from the shame, guilt and internal disquiet that compels their desire to dominate others.

Members of the BCM used these workshops as a blueprint for how to teach leadership skills to young people across the country. The emphasis on training their leaders to teach liberation thinking completely transformed the founding members' understanding of how the BCM could leverage its philosophy to promote permanent change in social relationships. The impact of this workshop was so profound that it changed the outlook of BCM members who would later receive second-hand accounts of the key principles.

While my mother would, over time, become one of Anne Hope's close friends, she did not attend those first training sessions. She was focused on completing her medical studies and leading the local SASO branch activities. She benefited from the feedback received from my father and others who had taken part in the workshops, learning through them an entirely new way of helping people in township and rural communities rethink their approach to their personal liberation.

In 1972, my mother's final year of medical school, she continued to lead the SASO Durban branch and relished the community engagements and work programmes that occupied most of her weekends. She describes 1971 and 1972, as the best years of the BCM, because the BCM leaders had finally found a way to integrate their sprawling ideas on Black Consciousness into a single internally coherent philosophy. Simultaneously, they had created the institutional vehicles to put the full suite of BCM principles into practice. In January 1972 Ben Khoapa was entrusted by Beyers Naudé's Christian Institute to manage funds to help counter the corrosive impact of apartheid in black communities. These funds were raised through the Dutch Reformed Church network. With the support of the South African Council of Churches, he started the Black Community Programmes, or BCP.

Uncle Ben was a MoSotho from Matatiele and had a master's degree in social work. During this period he was attached to the

Young Men's Christian Association, or YMCA. His broad worldly knowledge base enabled him to tap into real-world experience, and he was seen as someone who could be relied upon to always give good counsel. He was comfortable with people from all walks of life, using his sense of humour to make people feel comfortable even when discussing sensitive topics.

Uncle Ben was popular among the BCM core group, and he was a great admirer and dear friend of my father. By this time my father had long lost interest in medicine, and consequently in December 1971 he was academically excluded from medical school. Uncle Ben was certain that my father could lend political weight and his keen insights to the BCP and thus asked him to become programme director. Since he was available and motivated to build a new platform that focused on both Black Consciousness and the development of black self-reliance, my father accepted.

The headquarters of the BCP was at 86 Beatrice Street in Durban, while the SASO offices were in the United Congregational Church building behind the BCP offices.[27] Two months earlier, Barney Pityana had been elected president of SASO and Harry Nengwenkulu had become secretary-general. Harry was a natural leader and educator who had served as president of the Student Body Council of the University of the North. These gifted leaders were finally able to leverage off each other and the institutions they led to effect change on a national scale.

Uncle Barney wanted to ensure SASO's long-term sustainability by building its operating systems and administrative capacity. During this time Strini Moodley was the publications director for SASO. Though there were very few resources, the team made sure that Strini was able to travel around the country on a third-class train ticket and visit various campuses in order to advise on how to replicate the BCM message in ways that were tailored to different national student preferences.

In his role as programme director of the BCP, my father started a publication called *Black Review*. This was intended to counter the negative narrative of daily life in black communities, as encapsulated in the annual review of the South African Institute of Race Relations, in which blacks were peripheral. *Black Review* created an alternative and more balanced narrative of the black experience. It went further than merely reporting events in black communities; it also provided the necessary context to explain why these events were occurring in the first place.

According to the 1973 edition of *Black Review*, '1972 saw the springing up of associations such as Black Community Programmes, which played an important role in bringing together youth, religious, educational and cultural groups. This led to the creation of several associations which stood for the positive development of self-reliance in the black community.'[28]

These organisations began working together as a network representing the BCM. Though they each had separate leadership, they coordinated their organisational missions, acting as organs of advocacy, community outreach, positive propaganda and student politics. To the outside world, these organisations were separate and had different funders and governance structures. But because the leadership of these organisations was socially and philosophically integrated, the output that each institution generated was deftly coordinated.

The results were spectacular. From 1972 it became clear that black students would be in the vanguard of a movement that would one day lead black people to self-determination. These developments captured the attention of the ANC and PAC. Both organisations began internal discussions on how to respond to what these student leaders were doing. As the leader and main spokesperson for the movement, Steve Biko was becoming more articulate and radical in describing the change that black people sought. Over the coming months and years, both Oliver Tambo and Robert Sobukwe enlisted intermediaries to make contact with my father to discuss the possibility of working together.

While these political developments were unfolding, my mother was focused on doing well in her final exams. Upon completing her exams, she was required to do her internship at a designated hospital. On 2 January 1973 she was asked to report to King Edward VIII General Hospital in Durban. She remembers it as being overcrowded, filthy and dilapidated, but in those years this was par for the course due to the general disregard for black people.

My mother tells me she saw some horrific things at King Edward. In the paediatric ward, for instance, she often observed three infants in one cot. There was a constant shortage of staff and resources to tend to needy patients. Very often she would be infuriated by the lack of basic supplies for patients. Many of the wards simply did not have enough clean clothes or linen, which meant that patients often infected one another with diseases passed through germs trapped in linen or clothing. As far as she could tell, the professors who were supervising the interns at the hospital had become so accustomed to these inequities that they did not raise alarm bells. The level of racism that permeated public and private life during the 1970s allowed the senior doctors to mentally normalise what would, in a hospital for white people, be regarded as highly abnormal circumstances.

My mother stayed in a small single room in the doctors' quarters on the hospital property. She was grateful that at least this meant she and the rest of the interns didn't have to travel long distances to attend to their training. The interns ate mediocre food in the dining hall close by, after which my mother would retire to her spartan bedroom, which was more like a high-school dormitory room.

While my mother and her colleagues, such as KG Mokgatle, Ben Mgulwa, Xola Pemba, Goolam Abram and Chapman Palweni, stayed in the decrepit old doctors' quarters, white medical students at universities such as Wits, UCT, Stellenbosch and Pretoria were doing their internships in vastly different conditions. White interns lived in relatively plush quarters, got all the plum assignments and, to add insult to injury, were paid twice what black interns used to receive in those days. My mother recalls that at this time her take-home pay was around R200 per month.

After a long work week that often involved days without adequate sleep, my mother and her fellow black interns made sure they used Friday evenings, when they were not on call, to have some much-deserved fun. Xola Pemba, a giant man of Khoi descent, would be charged with collecting cash for beer and cheap wine. The alcohol, along with well-worn soul-music records, was enough to fuel house parties that would last long into the night.

Despite this Friday ritual, medical internship was physically gruelling and psychologically demanding. Regardless of the material differences between white and black interns, they worked together quite well. They were aware that they had received the same medical training, spent the same number of hours in the lab and doing hospital work, and as such were professional equals in each other's eyes.

What the white interns may not have appreciated was how difficult it had been for their black peers to get into the medical profession in the first place. They had no way of understanding the challenging circumstances of many of these black interns. My mother and Goolam Abram, whom she regarded as a brother, used to marvel at the incredible odds they had to overcome to make a success of their lives. My mother's resource-poor upbringing was the norm among black students; almost all of them had similar life experiences, which helped turn them into the compassionate doctors they became.

Mamphela remembers the arguments she had at tutorial meetings with Professor Edward Barry Adams, the head of the Department of Medicine, who was also the dean of the medical school. She regarded him as a conservative person with a condescending attitude to black people – patients as well as students. He had a tendency to ask his black students probing questions about the politics of the day. My mother refused to indulge him, saying simply, 'I don't discuss politics with people like you.'

Adams once told his colleague Professor YK Seedat, a good-humoured man, 'I don't want that woman in my section.' To this, Seedat, who was aware of my mother's disdain towards Adams, responded gleefully: 'The feeling is mutual.'

These real-world interactions outside the arena of student politics raised questions in the minds of many SASO members: what happens after they graduate? Do they stop participating in politics and retreat to normal lives doing ordinary jobs? This prospect was unfathomable for people who had spent the last three to six years deeply involved in robust student politics.

After intense discussions among some of the founding SASO members, who were by now all young professionals, two points of view emerged. People like Steve Biko thought that the BCM represented a cultural movement that did not need to fit into a party-political formation. Others believed that with the ANC and PAC banned, there was a desperate need for a political platform that would meet people's latent desire to confront the apartheid government more directly. This latter view carried the day. Even though my father and others were initially not in favour of this view, they accepted the decision and worked vigorously to help shape and guide the implementation of this resolution to create a political platform.

The launch of the Black People's Convention in July 1972 added a political wing to the BCM that would complement the activities of the BCP and SASO. Significantly, the first president of the BPC was the educational specialist Motlalepule Winifred Kgware. While other political parties saw fit to start women's leagues, the BCM differentiated itself by choosing women to take leadership roles in core organisational structures. Thus, within the BCM there was a clear division of labour: the BPC was the 'adult' political body, SASO the student political body, and the BCP was the community-projects arm.[29]

By 1973, the apartheid government had gathered enough information to decide that the BCM represented a major threat to the status quo in South Africa. On 26 February, the secretary-general of the Black Allied Workers' Union, and a founding member of the BCM, Drake Koka, and the Johannesburg-based reporter and BCM member Bokwe James Mafuna were banned for allegedly inciting union workers to violent protests.

On the same day, Steve Biko, Barney Pityana, Strini Moodley, Saths Cooper, Jerry Modisane (then SASO president) and Harry Nengwenkulu were banned for five years. This meant that they were restricted to the town they lived in, had restrictions on the number of visitors they could have and were subject to random police inspections. In August of that year, Mosibudi Mangena, chairperson of the SASO Pretoria branch (and later president of Azapo), was arrested and sentenced to five years in prison for allegedly recruiting two policemen to join the armed struggle. When these leaders were replaced by the next generation, another round of arrests followed in October 1973.

As soon as my father was banned and restricted to King William's Town, he called my mother and reminded her of their pact to never let anything separate them again. He suggested that she consider how she could make the transition from Durban to the eastern Cape Province. They agreed that she would fly to and from East London airport on weekends when her colleagues could cover her clinical duties in Durban.

Usually, fellow BCM member Malusi Mpumlwana would fetch her at the airport and bring her up to date on the latest BCM news during the drive to King William's Town. Uncle Malusi had left medical school in 1972. His medical career lasted for just one year, since he spent virtually no time at his books, instead immersing himself in all things BCM. Uncle Malusi had returned to live in Umtata in 1972, where he and his brother ran a small business. However, when he heard that my father had been banned he went to visit him in King William's Town and decided he was not going to leave.

Uncle Malusi was only allowed to stay in King William's Town for 48 hours due to pass-law regulations, but he discovered a loophole in the law. In the event that police would harass him when his 48-hour limit in the town was over, he would simply drive towards East London until he officially left the King William's Town area, do a U-turn and return with a fresh 48 hours to spare.

His formal job within the BCM was to work on the *Black Review* as a researcher and co-author of the book-sized annual publication, which consisted of reports on key events and challenges in the black community. He was joined in this work by Thoko Mbanjwa, a former liberal-arts student at Fort Hare, whose father was a parish priest of the Congregational Church in King William's Town. Over time, as the two worked together on the *Black Review*, they fell in love. Their relationship had none of the ups and downs of my parents; they instantly knew they were meant to be together and have, to this day, never let each other go.

From the middle of 1974, my mother applied to be transferred from King Edward VIII Hospital to Livingstone Hospital in Port Elizabeth to complete her internship. At Livingstone she began a second six-month internship – this time as a surgeon. Back then, Livingstone Hospital was a new and beautifully built provincial hospital with the latest facilities. It was well run and maintained by a dedicated, highly motivated leadership team. Compared to what my mother had been used to in Durban, the doctors' quarters were luxurious.

After she settled in Port Elizabeth, my mother would hitch-hike to King William's Town at least one weekend a month. In those days it was still relatively safe for a woman to hitch a ride. She remembers how she would wait close to the New Brighton power station near the highway and within minutes a compassionate stranger would give her a lift. A couple of hours later she would be dropped off in King William's Town. During this period, my father was staying at his mother's place in Ginsberg.

After his forced relocation to King William's Town, my father looked for an office to work from as the programme director of the BCP. During his search, he was introduced to a young, dedicated Anglican priest named David Russell, whose focus was on Dimbaza township, some 23 kilometres away. He lived in a cottage at 14 Leopold Street, next to an unused church building, and Father David duly requested the church authorities to make this building available to my father.

The two quickly found that they were interested in some of the same things and began enjoying long, engaging intellectual conversations. Though they didn't always agree on the topics they debated, the two men formed a healthy relationship. For example, my father questioned the priest's approach to welfare. He argued that while it was a good thing that Father David was sending old clothes to the people of Dimbaza, he thought this did not sufficiently advance the dignity of the people in this area.

With the help of Father David, my father soon set up offices for both SASO and the BCP in the old church at 14 Leopold Street. Through the BCP, my father supported the establishment of the Zimele Trust, which was to be led by Mapetla Mohapi. Its mission was to conscientise and mobilise former political prisoners. Mapetla, who came from the rural village of Jozanashoek in the former Transkei, was a courageous and energetic young BCM leader who had graduated with a degree in social work from the University of the North. He had a deep compassion for the traumatic experiences people went through while serving their sentences in South Africa's notoriously cruel prisons.

The Zimele Trust was a shining example of the practical manifestations of Black Consciousness. The work entailed helping former political prisoners with social reorientation and professional upskilling so that they could begin to create livelihood opportunities for themselves. It was important to both my father and Mapetla that the programme help to overcome the divisions between ANC and PAC members, which had hardened during their incarceration on Robben Island.

What they achieved through the Zimele Trust fulfilled the BCM's call for solidarity among liberation movements. In most cases, the former prisoners emerged from the experience conscientised to a new and more inclusive idea of political activism. The programmes run by the Zimele Trust were aimed at restoring the dignity of these former prisoners by assisting them with acquiring skills in carpentry, farming, leatherworking, retailing or other skills needed by businesses in the area.

My mother, who had been observing the BCP from a distance, was captivated by the wide-ranging social impact they could make. She had started to consider how she could make a contribution when she discovered she was pregnant. Given that her internship would end in a few months, the timing was quite convenient. My father was excited about the news, knowing that this would bring them even closer.

However, as her pregnancy went on, she developed a large fibroid on her uterus, which became very painful. She consulted doctors, who advised that she should have an operation to remove it. Once she recovered from the operation, her supervisors allowed her to finish her internship commitment at Livingstone Hospital at the end of 1973.

For the remainder of her pregnancy, Mamphela moved into the home of her Aunt Mamotsatsi Mabaso in Zola, Soweto, where her sister Mashadi was also living. Aunt Mashadi was then a senior nurse at Baragwanath Hospital and secured a room in the maternity ward for her. Aunt Mashadi was, and remains, a rock in my mother's life. She has always been generous in her support of her little sister, especially in my mother's times of greatest need.

My sister Lerato was born in May 1974. Mamphela briefly went to stay with her mother, Tsipu, in Maupe, where my grandmother was working as a teacher. Based on discussions between my mother and my grandmother, it was only a matter of time before my father would propose. The arrangement was that she would look after the baby to allow my mother time to start her career and begin earning much-needed money. However, my father's preference was for Lerato to be brought to Mamcete, but my maternal grandmother refused. Tsipu felt that the child could only live with my father when my parents were married and had their own home. As a man who knew African customs intimately, my father understood and respected Tsipu's wishes.

In July 1974 my mother got a job as a medical officer at Mount Coke Hospital, outside Zwelitsha township, near King William's Town. She would live in the doctors' quarters on the property. It was from this base that she was asked, on behalf of the BCM, to prepare for the opening of Zanempilo Community Health Centre, which had been conceptualised as a new primary-health-care centre during the course of 1973–1974. Preparatory work entailed drawing up specifications for furniture, equipment, drugs and other materials essential to running a functional community health centre with a maternity wing. It was quite a tall order for a young and inexperienced doctor, but everyone involved was learning on the job. They used whatever experience they had to lay the foundational elements of the practical manifestations of Black Consciousness.

Tragedy struck a few weeks later, in August, when my mother received a call informing her that Lerato had died of broncho-pneumonia. My parents were devastated. The death was made more difficult by the fact that my sister had died of a treatable illness.

Upon hearing the news, Malusi Mpumlwana fetched my mother and took her to Mamcete's house, allowing her to grieve with my father. Because of his banning order, my father and Mamcete decided that his elder brother, Khaya, would represent the family at Lerato's funeral. The following day Uncle Khaya and my mother flew to Johannesburg and travelled to Uitkyk to lay Lerato to rest.

I don't think my mother ever had the space to grieve her daughter's death properly. The death also caused serious strain in my parents' relationship, making an already complex situation even more intense. My father had promised to get a divorce, but after Lerato's death he began equivocating on his commitment to free himself for their marriage. As had happened before, they both sought refuge in their political activities. My mother returned to focus on preparations for the Zanempilo project launch, determined to make it a success.

Lawrence Msauli, a doctor in private practice in Mdantsane, guided Mamphela, giving her much-needed technical support in getting Zanempilo up and running. Msauli was a humorous, well-travelled man who called himself Lorenzo. He was introduced to my mother through the BCM network as a man with experience in building and running primary health-care facilities. To this day my mother wonders what she would have done without his help.

She readily confesses that at the time of Zanempilo's construction, she had no idea where to start with such a project. However, with the help of people like Lorenzo, the community health centre was completed on time and just under budget.

Zanempilo cost R30 000 to build, and its completion owed much to the help of a generous donor, a German South African called Angela Mai, who provided the capital by drawing on a portion of her inheritance that she couldn't take out of the country (the apartheid government blocked funds to stem capital outflow).The BCP, with the support of the Christian Institute, provided additional capital for furniture and equipment. Later, another donor provided R4 000 for the construction of a doctors' residence.

With these significant financial contributions, and an enormous amount of 'sweat equity', Zanempilo was officially opened in August 1975. My mother moved into the facility, using a bedroom designed for nurses on call and the adjacent staff room as a flatlet.

An able staff complement was picked from among the talented BCM activists within the network. Nontobeko Moletsane, a senior nursing sister whom my mother had met at Mount Coke, helped to recruit a nursing staff complement of five and to manage the many day-to-day functions. This enabled Mamphela to continue to multitask between acting as medical officer-in-charge and leading initiatives to promote community socio-economic development. The latter responsibilities would grow after the apartheid government tightened my father's banning order in late 1975, to preclude him from continuing his job with the BCP. My mother was asked by Ben Khoapa, the executive director of the BCP, to take on the additional responsibilities of programme director.

The apartheid era was marked by a gradual but systematic re-direction of budgets that shifted money away from the black townships that housed the majority of South Africans towards white urban and rural areas. By 1975, many black communities had been completely abandoned by the apartheid government and were in desperate need of help. To put things into perspective, the level of poverty in the King William's Town district was so severe during the 1970s that malnutrition was a common occurrence among the black population.

Nontobeko once recounted a harrowing story to my mother. While visiting a local family, she noticed the children crying on a blanket on the floor of the kitchen, looking miserable. When she asked why the children were crying and looked so drowsy, their mother told her she had nothing to feed them. She was boiling a pot filled with water just to give them hope that food would come, knowing they would fall asleep waiting.

Conditions such as pellagra (vitamin deficiency), kwashiorkor (severe protein malnutrition), marasmus (wasting away due to inadequate calorie intake) and stunted growth were common at this time. Many children died unnecessarily of diarrhoea, vomiting and other treatable diseases that accompany malnutrition and compromised immune systems. This level of abject material poverty and hunger was also not unique to the then eastern Cape Province.

Across the country, black families also had to live for months on end without the presence of males in the household due to the migrant labour system. This forced men to leave rural areas to go to work in the cities, abandoning their spouses and children, who were left to fend for themselves. As a consequence, the architects of apartheid to a great degree were successful in killing the institution of the black family.

Zanempilo Community Health Centre promoted social development that was rooted in self-liberation, moving from a sense of inferiority towards a more confident and assertive self-reliance that was the key to real empowerment. A vegetable garden was planted around the centre to show families how subsistence farming could alleviate hunger and promote good nutrition and food security.

A leather-manufacturing project was initiated at Njwaxa, between Alice and Dimbaza, to show people how enterprises were created and sustained to foster self-reliance. The leather-manufacturing facility was started with the support of Father Timothy Stanton of the Community of the Resurrection in Alice. He mobilised the required resources through the Church of England and Christian Aid, a British NGO. As the project grew, Aunt Bandi's husband, Mxolisi, was employed as project manager to handle quality control and marketing so that the leather goods could be sold at a fair price.

My mother's increasing workload led to the recruitment of Dr Siyolo Solombela, a dedicated activist from Butterworth (today eGquwa). In addition, Dr Msauli volunteered to do relief duties so that Mamphela and Dr Solombela could have some weekends off.

The Zanempilo Community Health Centre soon became the unofficial headquarters of the BCM. It was where BCM leaders met visitors and members of the media, and, most importantly, where they held internal meetings to plan their next moves. My father also met visitors at Zanempilo, which afforded greater privacy than the Leopold Street offices, where he was under constant surveillance by the security police. Uncle Malusi also spent a considerable amount of time running various special projects of the BCM out of Zanempilo.

On weekends there was time for fun and relaxation, which helped them maintain their deep, long-lasting friendships. Zanempilo offered a safe space that enabled the BCM activists, for the first time since their early days in Durban, to spend time together as a group, and to properly reconstitute themselves into a multipronged movement.

Throughout this period, my parents' relationship had its ups and downs. My father was indecisive, sometimes thinking he should get divorced and at other times feeling overpowered by his sense of duty towards Aunt Ntsiki. On top of his own

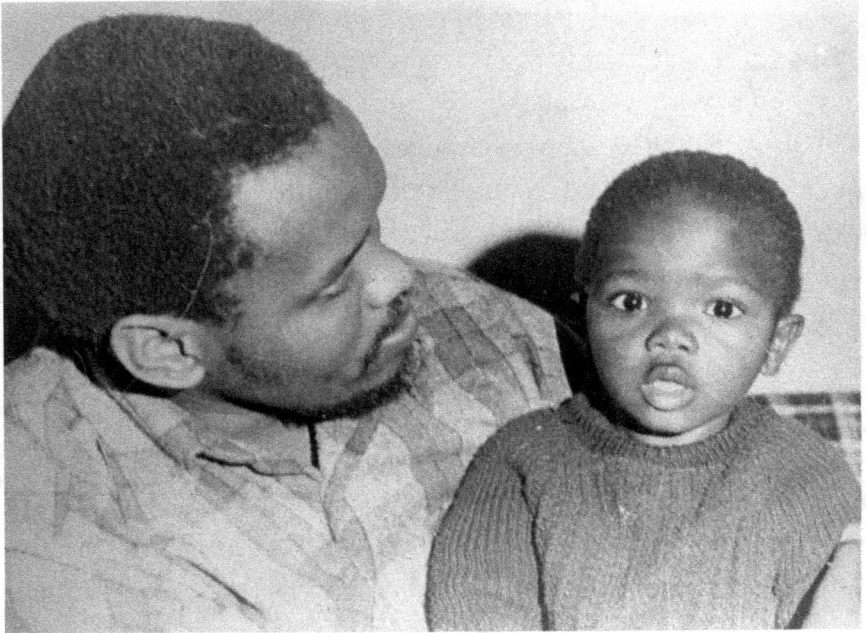

Steve Biko with his son Samora.
(Drum Social Histories/Baileys African History Archive/Africa Media Online)

trepidation, there were various social pressures not to get divorced. He loved Aunt Ntsiki and felt a deep sense of loyalty to her, which reinforced his inclination to stand by his marital obligations.

Shortly after Lerato's death, my father confessed to my mother that Aunt Ntsiki was pregnant. My brother Samora was born later in 1975. Though my father was very happy to have another son, my mother was heartbroken and felt that she might not be able to forgive him for going back on their agreement. These developments strained my parents' relationship almost to breaking point.

8

An unjust trial and unjustifiable murders

In 1974, following a revolution in Portugal, the decade-long Mozambican war of independence, between the guerrilla forces of the Mozambique Liberation Front (Frelimo), led by the brave and charismatic freedom fighter Samora Machel, and the Portuguese colonial army, came to an end. A ceasefire was announced on 8 September, effectively signalling the liberation of the Mozambican people.

To celebrate the ceasefire, and as a sign of solidarity with Frelimo, SASO and the BPC held rallies in Durban and at the Turfloop campus of the University of the North on 25 September. Saths Cooper planned and coordinated this protest action. By then, the banned leadership of the BCM had spread out all over the country and thus could not meet regularly, forcing them to become accustomed to indirect communication through emissaries. The prospect of Mozambique's independence prompted Uncle Saths to request my mother to get my father's support to launch a mass-action campaign designed to stir the South African population into more intensive mass action.

According to Uncle Saths, they deliberately avoided asking Barney Pityana because they knew he would calculate the risk they were taking and forbid the action on the grounds that too many people would be killed, hurt or jailed. Uncle Barney confirms that his inclination would have been to protect lives, but as he told the security police, who arrested him on suspicion of involvement in planning the Frelimo rallies, had he been in the debates he would no doubt have been convinced to participate in these rallies and would have given them his full attention.

In fact, unknown to Uncle Saths, Makhenkesi Stofile, a young BCM member (who would later become premier of the Eastern Cape province), was asked by Steve Biko to go to New Brighton in order to brief Barney Pityana on the general direction they were going to take. Uncle Barney's response was that he was too far removed from the organising team to make an informed decision. Though his inclination was to be careful, he was happy to rely on the instincts of those closer to the action.

Upon receiving the go-ahead from Steve Biko, Uncle Saths decided that the message at the rallies would be to focus South Africans' gaze on the looming freedom around the corner, and to follow the example of the citizens in our neighbouring countries. At this time, Angola too was poised to gain independence from Portugal, while the liberation struggle was building strength in South West Africa (today Namibia), then under South African administration.

Kogila Cooper, Uncle Saths's sister-in-law, remembers how a rally was organised at the Curries Fountain football stadium for 25 September: 'The "Viva Frelimo Rally" was planned to start at about 5.30 pm. When we got to the stadium, we found a huge crowd had already gathered and were singing and dancing peacefully. The police were also there in great numbers, some blocking the entrance to Curries Fountain with their vans. We were trying to find some of our BPC members when the police made an announcement on the loud-hailer declaring the meeting illegal and ordering the crowd to disperse. Nobody heeded this command, but carried on singing and dancing with their fists up in the black power salute.'[30]

Since mass gatherings of black people had been banned by the police, the rally predictably led to the arrest and detention of scores of BCM leaders. The state eventually charged nine of these SASO/BPC leaders, including Saths Cooper, Strini Moodley, Mosiuoa (Terror) Lekota and Nchaupe Maitshwe Mokoape, under the Terrorism Act on 31 January 1975. The two principal charges were conspiracy to bring about revolutionary change and the promotion of racial hostility.

In July 1975 the trial of the so-called SASO Nine, or the Black Consciousness Trial, began at the Pretoria Supreme Court. The defence's position was encapsulated in the following opening line from Uncle Saths's statement: 'We, the innocent, are being arraigned before this court for the crimes perpetrated by the white superstructure in this country.'[31]

The trial would last 23 months, becoming one of the country's longest political trials. Soon after the state ended its case and the defence presented its arguments, my father was called to testify in early May 1976. Despite being offered the option to fly, Steve Biko insisted on driving from King William's Town, which allowed him the chance to stop in many towns along the way to get a sense of where people's hearts and minds were. The week-long drive was followed by a four-week stay in Pretoria and Johannesburg while he waited to give his testimony.

By then he had been banned from speaking in public for three years, and there was great demand among the mass of South

Africans to hear him speak. In the introduction to a book of the transcripts of my father's testimony, editor Millard Arnold writes:

> On May 2, 1976, David Soggot, senior counsel for the defence in the trial of Sathasivan Cooper and Eight Others in Pretoria, South Africa, called to the witness stand Stephen Bantu Biko. A low murmur rolled across the crowded courtroom. Anxiety and anticipation caused most to squirm slightly in their seats. Steve Biko was to testify. No one knew it at the time, but it was to be the last public appearance Biko would ever make . . .[32]

Unwittingly, the apartheid government had given one of its chief opponents the opportunity and a public platform to present Black Consciousness as a fully developed philosophy. By most people's accounts, Steve Biko's four and a half days of testimony was the clearest, most coherent description of Black Consciousness. For many people, it was the first time they began to understand the essence of this philosophy.

It is not a coincidence that less than two months after his testimony, students in Soweto were stirred to massive protests in an event commonly referred to as June 16. The fact that 4 000 children were injured and hundreds killed in their effort to state that they loved themselves too much to submit to the superiority complex of the apartheid state is still the most unjustifiable of the apartheid regime's many crimes. These children were simply living the Black Consciousness philosophy as explained to them by Steve Biko. In several on-camera interviews my father did after 16 June, it is clear that the deaths of these children left an emotional scar that made him even more determined to devote himself – including, if needed, to give his life – to opposing the unjust regime.

During his testimony at the SASO Nine trial, my father outlined the rationale for BCM:

> Basically Black Consciousness refers itself to the Black man and to his situation, and I think the Black man is subjected to two forces in this country. He is first of all oppressed by an external world through institutionalised machinery: through laws that restrict him from doing certain things, through heavy work conditions, through poor education, these are all external to him, and secondly, and this we regard as the most important, the black man in himself has developed a certain state of alienation, he rejects himself, precisely because he attaches the meaning white to all that is good, in other words he associates good and he equates good with white. This arises out of his living and it arises out of his development from childhood . . . This is carried through to adulthood when the black man has got to live and work.[33]

As Saths Cooper and his colleagues faced numerous charges, they expected to be sentenced to at least ten years in prison. They were therefore pleasantly surprised when on 21 December 1976 they were sentenced to 'only' six years. Such was the chutzpah of the SASO Nine triallists that they actually celebrated this sentence as a moral victory. Two days later, the group found themselves on Robben Island. Uncle Saths was allocated a cell in the same block as Nelson Mandela the following year.

Life in prison was made difficult by the relentless effort of the prison system to break the spirits of these young rabble-rousers. According to Uncle Saths, by around March 1977 they had become accustomed to the routine of meaningless, mind-numbing work in the lime quarry, where they were under the constant threat of dogs being egged on by their handlers. In one instance, one of the SASO Nine was hit with the butt of an R1 rifle. Another sustained a foot injury inflicted by a pickaxe because the warders stupidly insisted that those who were shovelling the lime should continue to do so while others were pickaxing the hard rock face. They walked back to the prison in disgust carrying their injured comrade, leaving the warders and their baying dogs to run behind them.

As he relates the incident to me, Uncle Saths can't help but laugh when he recalls the name of the cordoned-off part of the prison they took their injured prisoner to: Swartmag Seksie (Black Power Section). The SASO Nine were such a nuisance on Robben Island that in January 1977 walls were built to divide the different sections of the prison to keep the group away from other prisoners. While these BCM leaders were growing notorious in the Swartmag Seksie, their fellow leaders on the outside were elevated to the rank of enemies of the state.

One of the consequences of becoming persona non grata in the eyes of the apartheid state was that you became a focus for the security police. Every single leader of the BCM was constantly watched. As Steve Biko, Mamphela Ramphele, Malusi Mpumlwana and local community leaders took concrete action to establish initiatives that actively promoted self-reliance among black people, they were increasingly putting themselves at risk, and the work they were doing was becoming more dangerous.

They were also aware that their actions were under constant surveillance and took every precaution not to be caught by the security police doing anything illegal. Yet, precisely because the stakes were so high, certain actions had to be taken to keep the momentum of their work going.

Saths Cooper at an Azapo meeting in 1983.
(Cedric Nunn/Independent Contributors/Africa Media Online)

Uncle Malusi told me of one such a dangerous mission to attend key meetings in Cape Town. When he arrived in the Cape he was chaperoned by a local BCM activist regarded by the apartheid classification system as coloured. On a Friday afternoon they were working in Langa township with a car packed full of pamphlets and other political documents. The next moment, they were pulled over by the police and were asked to get out of the car and show their documentation.

At this stage, each knew they had two different but equally serious problems. Uncle Malusi had no permit to be in a township outside his residential area. His colleague, by virtue of being designated coloured, was not allowed to be in a black township. To ensure they did not end up in even bigger trouble, they pretended to lose their car keys so the cops could not open and search their vehicle. They were taken to separate jails.

On his first night in jail Uncle Malusi was told by his cell-mates that they had been asked to beat him up to teach him a lesson. He told them who he was and began describing the BCM's core principles to his fellow prisoners. In no time they had organised a bottle of brandy to drink while they listened attentively to what he had to say. Uncle Malusi reciprocated by sharing a large meal that had been sent to the prison by a local BCM family from Langa. The weekend was thus spent singing struggle songs, talking politics and sharing stories about their lives.

On the following Monday a short black man who worked in the official role of 'friend of the prisoners' was sent to get the details of all those detained and offered to let their employers know where they were. Uncle Malusi explains that he became suspicious of the man when he attempted to advise them all to plead guilty so as not to get on the magistrate's wrong side. Uncle Malusi calmly explained everyone's rights to them; because of his help, the charges were later dropped and all of them went free.

When it was his turn to appear in court, Uncle Malusi was so fired up that when he was told by the court that a lawyer was there to assist him, he refused to meet this man. The case was dismissed, and Uncle Malusi had no way of knowing that he had turned down the help of Dullah Omar, a future minister of justice.

This was by no means the first time that Omar had helped members of the BCM. He also represented the SASO Nine while they were on Robben Island. Like many gifted legal practitioners who supported the struggle, he worked largely pro bono, taking satisfaction in fighting the unjust apartheid system through the courts.

A major reason for the increased scrutiny of the BCM was that the Soweto uprising had rocked the apartheid system to the core. The white-minority government was challenged by young people who were living the manifestation of the Black Consciousness philosophy. The imposition of Afrikaans as a medium of instruction in black schools by the minister of education, Andries Treurnicht, was the straw that broke the camel's back. Thousands of children took to the streets in peaceful protests, which were met with brutal police repression. In a panic, the government promulgated Section 10 of the Terrorism Act to allow for the detention of anyone who might be part of the broader resistance movement that was springing up across the country.

To add fuel to an already blazing fire, the founder of the Zimele Trust, Mapetla Mohapi, was killed in detention on 5 August 1976 at Kei Road police station. My mother had the unenviable task of attending his post-mortem at the local district surgeon's office with Dr Lawrence Msauli. She was devastated when their examination confirmed the suspicion that Mapetla's apparent suicide was a covered-up murder. Unfortunately for the family and the BCM, the security police had covered their tracks well and it was impossible for the two doctors, who were not professional pathologists, to prove any foul play.

After June 16, orders of detention were issued for everyone involved in the BCM nerve centre in King William's Town, as well as those in the rest of the country. Nor did the work taking place at Zanempilo escape the attention of the security police. The arrests were sudden and executed in a way that ensured BCM leaders were placed in different prisons. Those who were detained under Section 6 of the Terrorism Act (which determined that if an officer above the rank of lieutenant-colonel had a reason to believe that someone was a terrorist, they could be detained without trial), such as my father and Thenjiwe Mtintso, were held and interrogated for long periods. Mtintso, who went on to serve in the Top Six of the ANC as deputy secretary-general, was among those who were most brutally tortured.

Attempts to physically harm my father, who was held at East London police station, were stopped because of his forceful retaliation and clear verbal warnings to those about to touch him that he would defend himself and could not guarantee the outcome. The police resorted to verbal abuse and long periods of isolation. The police in East London were not above the rough treatment of prisoners, but they were wary of engaging in a physical scuffle with someone they knew would reciprocate both physically and legally. Like all bullies, they preferred to pick on easy targets.

My mother was the first to be detained under the newly proclaimed Section 10 of the Terrorism Act. She was taken to the new prison in King William's Town on the eve of Mapetla Mohapi's funeral in Herschel, near the Lesotho border. More women detainees followed, including Aunt Bandi and Thoko Mbanjwa. During this period, the various BCM leaders were each detained for up to four and a half months. Most of them believed that they would not be released any time soon, or, worse still, that they could be killed by the security forces. The life-threatening nature of their activism was by now a reality.

For many of the activists, this period of detention had the effect of bringing into focus their most serious life decisions. My father was released, after 101 days of detention, before Mamphela and his sister. Soon after his release, he went to visit my mother in the local prison. During this visit he told her that he had been thinking about what had taken place between them, and apologised for equivocating on making a final commitment to her. He explained that he was now ready to get divorced so the two of them could finally get married. This was music to my mother's ears.

Since my mother and Aunt Bandi were detained over the festive season, Mamcete sent a roasted leg of lamb and roast potatoes for them and the other detainees, who were held in a communal cell. Aunt Bandi and my mother spoke of their future as sisters-in-law and excitedly shared their dreams and fears, making vows to change their lives when they got out of jail. After coming face to face with death, many leaders resolved to live healthier, more family-oriented lifestyles. Some who had put off enrolling to further their education rededicated themselves to this task. Their close encounter with long-term incarceration, and the possibility of death, left them in a very reflective mood.

After my mother and Nobandile were released on 28 December, my mother's birthday, my parents had a long conversation. They agreed to forgive each other for things that had been said or done in the past and to find a place to live together as soon as possible. They spoke about the BCM and what actions needed to be taken in light of the state of the nation at the time. My father undertook to write a letter to my maternal grandmother to formally begin the traditional customs that precede African marriages.

Soon after the New Year, Aunt Ntsiki left the family household and went to work as a senior nurse in a hospital closer to her home in Umtata. My father also hired lawyers from his elder brother Khaya's firm to manage the formal divorce proceedings.

Though things between my father and Aunt Ntsiki had been strained for some time, she was heartbroken about the divorce.

My parents were not the only ones who were moved to get married by their experience in detention. Malusi Mpumlwana and Thoko Mbanjwa got married days after their release. Siyolo Solombela, one of my mother's colleagues at Zanempilo, also got married on the same day as the Mpumlwanas. They had all discovered that life was too short to miss even a single moment with the one you love.

Around this time, a house at the end of the street behind Mamcete's house in Ginsberg was on the market and my father purchased it in anticipation of settling there with my mother. At this point my parents began making plans to get married and take some time to establish their new family. My father sent a letter to Tsipu officially proposing to her daughter. Between December 1976 and April 1977, my parents shared some blissful time together, finally able to fully concentrate on their relationship. While there was a jovial and playful atmosphere within the BCM group based in King William's Town, they did not lose sight of the task ahead.

Unknown to many BCM leaders, my father had started to engage in clandestine conversations with the ANC. Oliver Tambo, the ANC's acting president, was interested in bringing the various BCM structures under the organisation's political machinery. These discussions were kept under the strictest of confidentiality, in part to prevent leaks, but also to create plausible deniability for other BCM leaders in case they were ever picked up by security police. A plane had been arranged to fly my father to Lusaka to have his first one-on-one meeting with Oliver Tambo. Because of the logistics involved, the meeting was planned months ahead of time. Sadly, circumstances conspired to postpone it.

Ahead of the planned meeting with Tambo, my father knew that he would have to deal with strong objections to collaboration with the ANC among members of the BCM in the then Cape Province. He also wanted to meet with Neville Alexander, the leader of the Unity Movement, a small Trotskyite political movement based in Cape Town that prided itself on its intellectually rigorous anti-apartheid analysis.

In parallel, equally secretive discussions were taking place with PAC leader Robert Sobukwe. Mapetla Mohapi (until his death in detention) and Malusi Mpumlwana served as the trusted intermediaries between Sobukwe and my father. Sobukwe and Biko shared a deep affinity with the goals and aspirations of each other's organisations. My father only took exception to the idea that, at that particular historical juncture, there was a need for a PAC separate from the ANC. My father believed that given the momentum established by the Soweto uprising, with the apartheid government on the ropes, it was time to unite all the significant anti-apartheid platforms. He felt that because of their established position and organisational structure, the ANC should be the vanguard of this new liberation front, even if he and Sobukwe and their organisations could add significant value.

This deft diplomatic mission required Uncle Malusi and Mapetla Mohapi to make numerous trips to Kimberley, where Sobukwe was restricted under the terms of his banning order. According to Uncle Malusi, Sobukwe was one of the most thoughtful and impressive men he has ever met. They would always convene with Sobukwe at his home, where they would deliver Biko's core messages. Then they would listen attentively to the views expressed and philosophical positions taken by Sobukwe, so that they could accurately report back. However, the security police got wind of these trips between Kimberley and King William's Town and began regular raids and arrests to curtail their freedom of movement.

With the security police's antennae now finely tuned to the BCM leadership's every move, surveillance in King William's Town was tightened. There were frequent raids on Mamcete's house to check on my father's whereabouts. Therefore my mother was not surprised when, one day in April 1977, several burly policemen arrived at the BCP offices at 14 Leopold Street and served her with a banning order. She was forcibly removed and driven to a police station without even being given a chance to pack any clothes. She was furious.

My mother received a five-year banning order that confined her to Naphuno, in the Tzaneen district. In another display of the security police's cruelty, they chose to restrict her to the hottest part of the Northern Transvaal (today Limpopo province). In its severity, her banning order was similar to that given to Winnie Mandela, who was sent to Brandfort in the Free State. By this time, my mother had been singled out as one of the key threats to the apartheid government, and they were determined to get her as far away from the BCM nerve centre in King William's Town as possible.

The security police had hoped that by isolating my mother far from her friends and family, she would become lonely and dispirited. She arrived in Tzaneen and was delivered to the nursing home of a local hospital, Meetse a Bophele, where she spent the first night. The following morning, with the assistance of sympathetic nurses, she found her way to the local headquarters of the Mission of the Sacred Heart, in Ofcolaco, southeast of Tzaneen, to seek help.

My mother explained to the perplexed Irish priests that she had been restricted to Naphuno and that she had no place to stay nor any resources to look after herself. Father Mooney, the head of the mission, welcomed her with open arms and let her use the telephone to let my father know what had happened to her and where she was. She was assured that she could stay with the local nuns in the village of Makhutswe for as long as she needed to.

Given her experience with arrests and the prejudiced nature of police work, Mamphela was not about to accept the banning order without a fight. Steve Biko asked Mziwoxolo Ndzengu, the reliable Zanempilo driver, to fly to Johannesburg and hire a car to take a suitcase of essential clothing and some money to my mother.

Three days after my mother's arrival, she received another visitor. A rickety VW Beetle arrived at Makhutswe bearing none other than Thenjiwe Mtintso, who was accompanied by a colleague. Thenjiwe and my mother had a raucous time, laughing and catching up on the latest news, before the visitors departed for Johannesburg at sunset.

Meanwhile, my father had arranged for a lawyer, Raymond Tucker, to visit my mother at Ofcolaco a few days later. Tucker carefully combed through the banning order, confirming that my mother's name had been spelled incorrectly and that the police also had the wrong identity number for her. My mother had pointed out these mistakes to the police but they had carelessly corrected them by hand. These mistakes rendered the banning order null and void.

Mamphela needed no further prompting after receiving Tucker's legal opinion. She went back to Makhutswe, where she found her brother Malesela waiting to see her so he could report to the family about how their sister was doing and get the details of her banning order. Malesela was told by his sister to make himself at home and get something to eat because they were about to set off for Rosettenville, Johannesburg. My mother planned to ask Father Stubbs to drive her to King William's Town. The universe conspired to provide storm cover as they left Tzaneen. Mamphela's security-police watchers would have assumed that she was safely in Makhutswe.

Father Stubbs could not believe his eyes when my mother knocked on his door at the Community House in Rosettenville. The trip to King William's Town gave them the opportunity to catch up on many of the happenings in the country and allowed Father Stubbs time to encourage my mother to think about beginning her own spiritual journey.

The long journey also offered my mother the opportunity to explain to Father Stubbs the full nature of her relationship with my father, where it had started, and how much they each had sacrificed. This served to convince Father Stubbs that as much as he was uncomfortable with the idea, Steve Biko had the right to divorce in order to pursue his happiness. There was shock but also much jubilation when they arrived at Zanempilo on a Friday afternoon, exactly a week after Mamphela had been forcefully removed from Leopold Street. The BCM leaders partied particularly hard that weekend, crowning it with a press scoop in the *Daily Dispatch* on Monday, announcing that Mamphela was back. The incompetence of the security police in issuing an incorrect banning order allowed my parents to spend a blissful two weeks together, a time during which I was conceived.

The security police had to apologise for their rudeness and shoddiness in the initial process. But the inevitable happened, and they wasted no time in issuing a corrected banning order that compelled my mother to return to Tzaneen. She was treated with much more respect this time. They even allowed her to drive her own car, assisted by Mziwoxolo, and found her a house in Lenyenye township, where she was to stay.

The Catholic Church arranged for Makgatla Mangena, the 16-year-old daughter of one of the parishioners in Makhutswe, to stay with my mother. The mother-daughter bond formed from the outset between these two women created a lasting mutually supportive relationship that continues to this day. Selema Masekela, father of the musician Hugh Masekela and my mother's uncle, was one of the first people to come and visit her, doing everything he could to keep her spirits high. Tsipu and my mother's siblings visited her regularly during those early days in Lenyenye.

In June 1977 my mother returned to King William's Town on the pretext that she was a witness who had to testify in a case that involved my father's breaking a banning order. By that time she had already reported to my father by phone that she was pregnant, so this offered my parents the opportunity to catch up and share the joy of the coming new life. Given the painful ordeal Steve and Mamphela had undergone with her last pregnancy, they could hardly believe they were going to have another chance to become parents.

Steve Biko and Mamphela Ramphele excitedly shared a week together discussing politics, catching up on news about their friends and talking about their new family. Like many couples in love, they thought their time together would last forever. They were both barely into their thirties and had no reason to expect that that week would be the last they would ever share.

At the time, they both thought that once my father's divorce was finalised and they could get married, the apartheid government would be legally bound to adjust my mother's banning order so that she could live with her husband. In light of this, they were light-hearted about their separation, their hearts and minds firmly focused on a future that they believed beckoned just over the horizon.

9

Sprout

I was born under truly strange circumstances. In fact, I almost died on the same day as my father.

A week before my father's death, my mother began to experience acute lower-abdominal pains. She sought help at Shilubane Hospital, in the next village from Lenyenye, where she was subsequently admitted. On the morning of 11 September 1977 her condition worsened and she was transferred to the provincial hospital in Pietersburg (today Polokwane). My due date was not until January 1978, so my mother knew that the pains were not labour but signs of trouble.

On the way to the provincial hospital she was filled with a sense of foreboding. As a doctor, she knew all the possible things that could be going wrong inside her body. She feared the worst but fought hard to hold on. When she arrived at the hospital she was admitted to a unit where a specialist obstetrician and gynaecologist was waiting to receive her. For a while there was no clarity on whether she would be able to keep the baby. Thankfully, the doctors managed to stabilise her. She was put on strict bed rest, with the foot of the bed elevated to take the pressure off her lower body. For an energetic workaholic like my mother, this was torture.

Almost as soon as she had arrived in Lenyenye, Mamphela had busied herself with establishing Ithusheng Community Health Centre, following the same community-transformation model as at Zanempilo. In a short time she created a strong network of health workers and community activists who enthusiastically supported the plans she presented to them.

My mother had been notified by friends a few weeks earlier that my father had been picked up by the security police on 18 August at a targeted roadblock set up between Port Elizabeth and Grahamstown.

Steve Biko had ignored his banning order to attend a set of important meetings in Cape Town that were meant to pave the way for his planned meeting with Oliver Tambo. According to Uncle Saths, at least one person in the Cape Town network was a government spy, and Dullah Omar later reported that this person had tipped off the security police. After my father had taken the risk of travelling to Cape Town by road, Neville Alexander waited until he had arrived in Cape Town before informing him that he would not see him. Uncle Saths recalls that while they were on Robben Island, Nelson Mandela told him that the ANC too had been heavily infiltrated and as a result operated under severe constraints.

My father and his colleague Peter Jones had to return to the eastern Cape without attending any of the meetings that had been set up. Peter was driving when they encountered a police roadblock outside Grahamstown. The two men almost made it through, but a faulty boot, of all things, exposed them. The police asked Peter to open the boot, but when it wouldn't open, their suspicions were raised. They began to look more closely at the car and at the two men in it. It was then that they realised that they had caught Steve Biko. Peter and my father were promptly arrested and taken to Port Elizabeth, where they were detained.

The interrogation process started with Peter, who was severely beaten and tortured to give the security police information about the trip and any other information about him and the BCM. Early in September they turned their attention to my father. The security police tried to beat a confession out of him. However, he refused to be humiliated and fought back until he was beaten into submission by at least ten security policemen. On 6 September, my father suffered three brain lesions that resulted in a massive brain haemorrhage.

He was seen by different doctors, who should all have recognised the signs of severe brain damage, but they did nothing to help or protect him. It was finally agreed that he should be transported to a prison hospital in Pretoria. On 11 September he was put in the back of a police van and driven, naked and barely breathing, to Pretoria.

At the exact time my father was dying in the back of a police vehicle, my mother and I were fighting for our lives in another vehicle en route to Pietersburg Provincial Hospital.

To make these coincidences even stranger, Uncle Barney, who was also in detention at that time, told me that on the night of 11 September, he dreamt that my father was asking him to take care of his children. He remembers asking my father, 'What makes you think your children will need to be taken care of?' As often happens in dreams, the question was left unanswered. He woke up with a sense of foreboding that something bad was about to happen to his friend.

On the morning of 12 September, my mother received a phone call. Given her doctor's strict order for bed rest, the nursing sister in charge had some trouble in convincing her to take the call in the staff room. When she picked up the phone, Thenjiwe Mtintso was on the line. Thenjiwe broke the news to her that the man whose child she was expecting, and whom she was about to marry, had been killed.

My mother returned to her bed in shock. Very little of what she was told made sense, and the rest of the day was a blur. When she woke up the next day, the morning newspapers carried the story of my father's death as the headline story. When she recalled that day, 42 years later, she told me that the phone call temporarily gave her the strength to keep her baby and fight even harder to get well. All she could think about was not losing her last remaining connection to my father.

A prison guard sneaked Uncle Barney a copy of one of the day's newspapers. His heart broke when he saw the headline. He went on a hunger strike and almost died from a combination of grief and lack of nourishment. The next few weeks were some of the hardest my mother and Uncle Barney would ever experience.

From the day my mother entered hospital in early September 1977 she had to spend almost two months in bed. As a result, she could not join the more than 20 000 people who travelled to King William's Town from all corners of the country, and many parts of the world, to pay their respects to Steve Biko. Uncle Barney remembers how a security policeman came to his cell and gleefully declared that he was going to miss 'one of the biggest political funerals in history'.

Such was the cruelty of the apartheid system that it is debatable if my mother would even have been allowed to travel to King William's Town for the funeral if she had been healthy. After all, she was still a banned person and restricted to the Tzaneen area. On top of not being able to bury my father, my mother found out that Aunt Ntsiki, who had been living separately from my father for almost a year with their divorce proceedings in the final stages, was taking up her role as his widow.

My mother was, of course, not the only one who was in pain. Malusi Mpumlwana planned my father's funeral despite losing his own father in the same week. Earlier that year, Uncle Malusi had been arrested and severely tortured. After his release, he confided to his friends that he had survived by finding a way to completely withdraw into himself. This deep trancelike state allowed him to block out the beatings and electrocution. He emerged from prison an even more spiritually attuned man.

When Desmond Tutu, at the time Bishop of Lesotho, was informed about Steve's death he excused himself from his duties to preside over my father's funeral. He began his eulogy with the following words: 'When we heard the news that Stephen Biko is dead, we were struck numb with disbelief . . . Oh, God, where are you? God, do you really care? How can you let this happen to us? It all seems such a waste of a wonderfully gifted person. Struck down in the bloom of his youth . . .' Those who know Desmond Tutu would realise that it takes a lot for him to question God and God's reasoning.

A dark fog hovered over the lives of many of my father's family members, friends, fellow activists and supporters as they tried to comprehend the inhumane actions that had taken Bantu Biko's life away. My father was one of countless young men and women who fell victim to the brutality of the apartheid security forces. He was the 46th political detainee to die during interrogation since 1963 when the government introduced laws permitting imprisonment without trial.[34]

To this day, the children and the grandchildren of these detainees live with the reality of a single-parent household and are left

Top: Steve Biko's coffin, bearing his carved likeness and the initials of the BPC, King William's Town, 12 September 1977.
(Drum Social Histories/Baileys African History Archive/Africa Media Online)

Bottom: Mourners follow the ox-cart carrying the coffin of Steve Biko, 12 September 1977.
(Drum Social Histories/Baileys African History Archive/Africa Media Online)

to pick up the pieces by themselves. A prime example is the recent case against the former Security Branch member João Rodrigues, who was tried for the death in detention of anti-apartheid activist Ahmed Timol. I was surprised to learn that the State Attorney's Office continues to pay his legal costs, while Timol's family gets no support. In May 2021 the judge in the matter officially noted his concern about this when Rodrigues appeared in court again.[35]

The massive uprisings that followed my father's death created panic and fear among the National Party leadership. As a result, a blanket order was issued on 19 October that banned any and every activity that had anything to do with the BCM. This led to mass detentions and the closing down of all BCM programmes and activities.

In many ways this was the ultimate tribute to the BCM leaders' comprehensive development approach to self-reliance among black people. At the height of the BCM, these programmes employed dozens of people and plans were afoot to expand the Njwaxa leather-manufacturing project, which would have employed several hundreds more. A new BCP health centre at Adams Mission, in Natal, called Impilo Community Health Centre, had been completed, and the furniture and equipment were about to be delivered and fitted in preparation for the launch of another comprehensive health-care programme.

These programmes proved that Black Consciousness was a prerequisite to a realisation of self that leads to a natural assertiveness in black people's interaction with white people. If South Africans were true to Steve Biko's vision of this country, they would retain a vested interest in promoting black people's capacity for self-respect and assertiveness. The country would join in helping black people channel their energy towards a renewal of their own communities. Government would follow, not lead, these initiatives.

The success of the BCM was in demonstrating that the progression from consciousness to self-realisation to assertiveness is the same for any ethnic group on planet Earth. It is only in a racist society that it would seem controversial for Africans to attempt to embark on this journey to escape the custodianship of white people.

Months after my birth on 19 January 1978, the pain of my mother's loss finally crystallised and she almost died from grief. The realisation of the extent of her loss, after all the sacrifices she had made, was almost too much to bear and she went into a deep depression. Besides the pain she felt for herself and the emotions of bereavement she had to endure, my mother was most saddened by the loss the country faced with the departure of Steve Biko from the political landscape.

If it was not for the spiritual and emotional support provided to her by acquaintances, friends, comrades and family, she would not have made it. She was blessed to have Father Thomas Duane of the Mission of the Sacred Heart sit at her bedside every day for the better part of two weeks after my father's death. Father Duane remained a close support to her, both spiritually and materially, for several decades. Father Timothy Stanton of the Community of the Resurrection also paid her regular visits in the first few months after my father's death.

Bishop Tutu not only phoned her weekly but also arranged funding through the offices of the South African Council of Churches, of which he was then secretary-general, for the Ithusheng Community Health Centre she had built at Lenyenye. On his many visits to Lenyenye, Uncle Malusi did his best to keep

her up to date with BCM developments and with what was happening in their friends' lives. From these visits and reports in
the media, Mamphela got a sense of the mood in the country.

At the beginning of 1978, my grandmother Tsipu took early
retirement to come and live with her daughter in Lenyenye. My
mother's two younger brothers, Thomas and Molepo, later joined
my mother's household. This network, and the endless stream of
supporters and comrades, kept her alive during what were her
darkest days.

The combination of her banning order and isolation from the
rest of the BCM founders, together with the loss of her husband-
to-be, threatened to break my mother. It was during this trying
time that her Christian faith was cemented, giving her a remark-
ably positive disposition that she has sustained all these years.
Learning to embrace God's presence through Christianity helped
my mother find the courage to prevail over her tragic circumstances. From the wise counsel she received from men and women
of the cloth, she was blessed with the wisdom to make sense of
what she had been through.

My mother's loss, first of my sister and then of my father,
heightened her anxiety about possibly losing me. Every mother
fears for her children, particularly in their early years. Her
anxiety and near neurosis regarding my welfare was at a whole
different level, though. If I was playing outside and she heard a
car coming, she would run out to check that I was safe. She was
always on the lookout to avoid any dreadful accident happening
to her infant child.

Because I was born during such a deeply tragic period in my
mother's life, family members were a constant feature around the
house. Every evening, at least one new person dropped in to check

on my mother. Tsipu was there, of course, and friends of Thomas and Molepo often came over for lunch or dinner. During holidays the rest of the Ramphele clan descended upon Lenyenye and I got to know my cousins. It didn't hurt that both my mother and Makgatla Mangena are unbelievable cooks. It's not surprising, therefore, that these visits often coincided with meal times.

When I was nine months old, my paternal grandmother, Mamcete, insisted that the family find a way to get me from Lenyenye to King William's Town. She wanted to meet her grandson, and to make sure that a family ritual called *imbeleko* was conducted. *Imbeleko* entails different things for different families, but it is the way Bantu people welcome a new member of the family into the world. In our case it involved the slaughter of a goat from the family kraal, a piece of which the child had to be helped to eat. A tendon from the leg of the goat was then dried and left in the container of the child's clothes as a ceremonial way to connect the child with the ancestral family.

Mamcete and my maternal grandmother, Tsipu, had become friends through correspondence. Their children had brought them together, but, as they would later discover whenever they spent time in each other's company, they were kindred spirits. From the time my father formally proposed to my mother in a long letter he wrote to Tsipu, her relationship with Mamcete as *mkhozis*, or in-laws, was cemented.

Since my mother was still subject to a banning order, she was not allowed to travel. Lenyenye is about as far from King William's Town as any place in South Africa, so driving a nine-month-old baby was out of the question. It was decided that I would be put on a flight with Sis Makgatla Mangena.

I was too young to remember the journey, but it has been described to me so often by so many people that it has inserted itself into my memory. What is important to note is that Sis Makgatla had never been on an aeroplane before. The flight on a propeller plane from Tzaneen to Johannesburg went smoothly, but the first drama was in Johannesburg when Sis Makgatla realised she could not carry both the baggage, which had to be checked in again for the flight to King William's Town, and a baby. When someone offered to carry me, she tightened her arms around me in a panic, thinking what my mother would do to her if she returned to Lenyenye without me.

But she finally managed to get us and our luggage checked in and we caught a connecting flight to East London. For some reason, she did not realise that we had to disembark when the plane landed. Instead, we remained on the plane, which took off for Port Elizabeth. When Sis Makgatla and the crew finally realised the mistake, they arranged for us to return on the same flight to East London.

Back in East London, Aunt Bandi had earlier watched in terror when our baggage was offloaded but we failed to disembark. Fortunately, she decided to wait and about two hours later we arrived. The trip was a complete nightmare for Sis Makgatla, who, on top of everything else, had to deal with a crying infant.

Once we reached King William's Town, we were engulfed in family love. Mamcete had baked her famous scones. As always in her house, prayers were said and then people were fed. My elder brothers, Nkosinathi and Samora, were present to share their first moments with me. My father's elder brother, Khaya, doted on me, as did many of the elders who passed me around the group of seated adults. The family rituals were performed and a bond was formed that would leave an indelible mark on my life.

The *imbeleko* ceremony must have been strange to an infant. With all the singing, dancing, chanting, praying and drinking,

I am certain I must have been terrified. Uncle Malusi would later explain why livestock are so symbolic in African traditional ceremonies. When a man is circumcised, for instance, the ceremony is performed near his paternal home so that his foreskin can be buried in the backyard with the foreskins of the entire male lineage. The family's cattle and other livestock usually graze in the backyard of the family home. Consequently, when a family pays dowry to another family, the cattle that are given to the woman's family carry more than symbolic meaning. The cattle are the first way in which the two families become united. When we had my *imbeleko*, the symbolism of the goat was that it, too, had grazed in the ancestral kraal, so it formed the first bond between me and my fellow clansman, oXhamela.

From the day I was born, Uncle Malusi has been around for every important moment in my life. He named me soon after my father's death by changing a popular Xhosa verb, *ukuhlumela* (which means 'to sprout'), into the noun Hlumelo (a sprout). He later explained the significance of the name: 'Sometimes when an old, large tree falls over and dies, green shoots or sprouts come out of the tree. You are one of those sprouts.'

10

Born at the right time

In as much as there may have been chaos, sadness and anxiety around my birth, as a child I had no inkling that this was my reality. What I saw growing up as a rural child was completely the opposite. I had an amazing first five years of life. My mother bought a house across the road from the brand-new Ithusheng Community Health Centre (ithusheng is a Sotho word that means 'help yourselves'). At first the centre had just five employees. Over time, though, it was expanded to launch a childcare centre, sustainable vegetable gardens, a brick-making and builders' training facility, a library and a youth development programme. A few years later, my mother recruited the talented Dr Lelau Mohuba from the University of the North to help her run the medical side of the clinic. This core group helped provide first-rate health care in a rural community that had never had such a luxury.

Both on the Ithusheng grounds and across the road in our small yard, the gardens that were planted afforded me and my friends access to mangoes, litchees, pawpaws, tomatoes, carrots, avocados and mealies. These grew in such abundance that no one could keep track of what we children ate during the day and what was expected as a crop yield. The only person we knew had to be on

Dr Mamphela Ramphele attends to a patient at the Ithusheng Community
Health Centre, Lenyenye.
(Alf Kumalo Family Trust/Africa Media Online)

our side was the custodian of those foods, the talented Moshothli
Mankgela, the landscaper and gardener. Apart from being happy
to look the other way as we plundered his garden, he was truly
a remarkable man. Born to a family with no financial resources,
Mankgela was differently abled as a child due to untreated club
feet. As a result, he lost the use of his legs, and had since childhood moved around using the power of his arms. He loved

children and spent a lot of time trying to teach us what he was doing in the garden. We listened politely until he gave us what we were really looking for – more litchees, pawpaws and mangoes.

My friends were the children of Mankuba Ramalepe, one of the senior nurses at Ithusheng, and were roughly the same age as me. Thabo, Tshepo and I were an inseparable trio. In the summer, we would get a kick out of stealing an egg from my mother's house and literally frying it on the pavement at noon, when the temperature would peak at 40–43 degrees Celsius. We enjoyed family picnics at nearby heritage sites such as The Chuenes, Echo Caves, The Downs and God's Window. Our birthdays attracted the attendance of what seemed like the entire village. We felt spoilt and well looked after. Every single friend and family member who visited my mother was sure to bring us sweets or other treats.

For a child, life in Lenyenye was idyllic. Village people in Limpopo have such a gentle manner about them, particularly towards little children. I would be welcome in any home on our street. As the uninvited, always barefoot child who wandered off the street into their homes, I enjoyed the simple hospitality that village people so dutifully offer to every visitor. With this sense of abundance, it hardly dawned on me that people who visited our three-bedroom home in Lenyenye would consider my family poor. I don't remember wanting for anything during my first five years of life.

My mother's brothers were lanky giants. None of them was under six feet tall. They were mostly calm and peace-loving, especially to me and my cousins Morongoa, Mpho, Nonoshe, Pitsi, Sethiba and Palesa, who also grew up with me in Lenyenye. The first time I realised that my uncles were not angels was when I was awoken in the middle of the night by a loud clank, which was the sound of my piggy bank breaking. As I rushed to turn on the light, I saw one of my uncles, clearly drunk and stumbling around, attempting to gather and stuff into his pockets the coins that represented my hard-earned savings. In retrospect, it was one of the funniest things anyone could witness. Caught red-handed, all my uncle could do was to plead for my silence and complicity in his scheme, which involved using all the money I had to buy one or two beers that night.

With all these men in the house I remember that I would some-times, in our quiet moments together, work up the nerve to ask my mother a question that we both had difficulty talking about. Where was my father? She took out a photo album with pictures of my father and then explained that he had been arrested by the same type of policemen who frequented our home, and that they had killed him. My mother remembers my hugging her and saying to her at that moment, 'Ag shame, mama.' After a few pensive moments I would ask to go and play outside.

She later explained that he was no longer in this world and that he was in heaven. She tried to describe this 'heaven' to me, and I remember not understanding why, if heaven was such a good place to be, the three of us were not there together. I once asked her why she didn't have a ring from my father, like some of the other women I had seen in Lenyenye, and she told me that I was her ring. These were difficult answers for a five-year-old to com-prehend. I think somewhere along the way I made a pact with myself not to put either of us through the trauma of having to ask and have her answer these questions. I would focus on what was there in the form of my mother's family and try not to think about what I didn't have.

While I was enjoying this simple and peaceful upbringing, the national reality of violence and despair was not lost on Barney Pityana and Mamphela Ramphele. In the late 1970s and into the

1980s, the brutality of the apartheid government's 'total onslaught' only succeeded in uniting black people's opposition to oppression. The result was a coordinated campaign of mass action intended to make South Africa ungovernable. In 1983 the formation of the United Democratic Front (UDF) saw churches, civic organisations, trade unions, sports bodies and student organisations pick up the mantle from the BCM by joining hands in opposing apartheid. Officially launched by delegates from 565 organisations, the UDF brought with it a more militant stance against apartheid, calling for the implementation of the Freedom Charter's vision for a non-racial, democratic country that belongs to all who live in it. Though the UDF attempted to draw in Mamphela Ramphele, she did not feel intimately connected to the politics they stood for.

Several months after my father was killed, Barney Pityana was finally let out of prison, though he remained under surveillance. Many of the people he bumped into told him that the security police would attempt to kill him if he stayed in South Africa any longer. Despite qualifying as a lawyer and spending a period of time as a legal clerk, with a right to appear in court, Barney Pityana decided that he would yield to a calling to become an Anglican priest. He applied to King's College London, to study theology, and was accepted. After his theological studies at King's College, Pityana would attend Ripon College Cuddesdon, near Oxford, where he underwent training for life in the Anglican ministry.

Shortly after he arrived in London, he was contacted by Oliver Tambo's office. Both Thabo Mbeki and Oliver Tambo sought to really understand Black Consciousness, its philosophy and its practical manifestations. Thabo Mbeki, in particular, had made it his business to read all of Steve Biko's and Barney Pityana's

Barney Pityana, July 1982.
(Drum Social Histories/Baileys African History Archive/Africa Media Online)

writings. Mbeki believed that there were some unique political and philosophical innovations that the ANC could learn from the BCM.

Charles Sibisi and his family emigrated to the UK soon after my father was killed. Uncle Charles's last job in South Africa was at the uMzimkhulu Psychiatric Hospital in Transkei. In the UK he took graduate courses to become a qualified psychiatrist. Through a stroke of fortune, Charles Sibisi and Barney Pityana lived in the same apartment building in Clapham, South London. This gave the two men and their families a measure of familiarity in an otherwise foreign country.

In 1980, an ANC delegation led by Alfred Nzo sought an audience with all the Black Consciousness alumni who could gather at the ANC office in Lusaka. Uncle Barney led the BCM delegation, which he said was well received. They met many former BCM colleagues who were by now deeply embedded in the ANC exile operations. It was resolved after this meeting that Pityana would convene a follow-up meeting in London to seek a mandate that would lead to more formal discussions in line with Steve Biko's earlier aspiration of unity in opposition to apartheid.

To say that Uncle Barney received a chilly reception from his colleagues in London would be an understatement. The meeting broke up into factional isolationist squabbles, permanently souring Pityana's appetite for BCM politics. Many BCM people who had been in exile for an extended period of time had changed their frame of reference towards the ANC, while others wanted nothing to do with ANC politics. Reconciling these two groupings proved impossible.

In South Africa, my mother was approached by the founders of Azapo to join hands with them in their movement to attempt to breathe life into what remained of Black Consciousness. She could not recognise any progressive instincts among the people who came to see her. They repeated Steve Biko's slogans without, according to Mamphela, a clear strategy to advance the underlying BCM agenda. My mother made up her mind that she would focus on implementing the practical manifestations of Black Consciousness in the communities where she worked. Though she supported what the UDF were doing, she opted to stay away from their political action campaigns.

Mamphela never enjoyed formal party politics and the realpolitik that necessitated cunning, plotting and alliance-building. She was having tremendous success in changing the mindset of the villagers she worked with from one of welfare to self-reliance.

Between 1981 and 1982, my mother continued to work as a community health practitioner but she studied part-time at Wits

Dr Mamphela Ramphele, January 1982.
(Drum Stories/Baileys African History Archive/Africa Media Online)

University to develop a speciality in tropical diseases. This integrated approach to wellbeing and conscientisation was to become her lifelong mission.

At home Mamphela was, like Tsipu, a strict disciplinarian. She wanted order and routine to reign both at work and at home. Everything had to be done in the most efficient, logical way possible. She was not above beating me if I tested her patience too much. As a result, I was raised in an orderly household where I was given the stability and predictability required to succeed. This home-based stability compensated for an external world in which I was constantly exposed to change. Throughout my upbringing, we moved house often. Sometimes we moved between countries; we also moved between villages and cities, for example when we left Lenyenye for Port Elizabeth, when I was five. This move followed my mother's appointment to Livingstone Hospital, which was sparked by her chasing a second opportunity at love.

While my mother was in Lenyenye she met and fell in love with Sipho Magele, a handsome pharmacist who was a lecturer at the University of the North. They decided to get married in 1982. On 16 March 1983 my little brother, Malusi, was born as the spitting image of his father. Magele had previously been married to Manana Kgware, daughter of Motlalepule Winifred Kgware (the first president of the BPC). Before they got divorced the couple had had two beautiful daughters.

In August of 1984, a year after the lifting of my mother's banning order, my mother, my brother and I moved to Port Elizabeth to stay with Magele. To be more accurate, he actually moved into the doctors' residence at Livingstone Hospital. He had not disclosed to my mother that he was struggling financially because of over-commitment and an unsustainable lifestyle. Though his financial struggles were neither here nor there as far as my mother was concerned, Magele's feelings of insecurity and bruised ego, the product of his financial dependence on his new wife, combined with his own violent nature, meant that, sadly for Mamphela, he turned out to be a psychologically abusive and irresponsible husband. By the end of October 1984 my mother had had enough and we moved cities again, landing in Cape Town. They divorced shortly afterwards.

I have to confess that those were the worst few months of my life. I tried to put on a brave face for my mother and brother, but I never got along with Sipho Magele. I was delighted to have a little brother and lasting close relationships with Magele's other children, but I remember myself being an enthusiastic packer when we were preparing to leave Livingstone Hospital. At this time Mamphela was fortunate enough to find a job working in a research institute at UCT, the Southern Africa Labour and Development Research Unit, or SALDRU, headed by the economist Francis Wilson.

Because of this bizarre set of circumstances, we only lived in Port Elizabeth for three months before moving to Cape Town, where we stayed with my mother's old Zanempilo colleague, Nontobeko, her husband, Tamsanqa Moletsane, and their delightful children. Mfundisi Moletsane ran a well-attended Anglican church in Langa. In Langa, we squeezed into the parish house on the property of St Cyprian's Anglican Church. The Moletsanes had four children, and though we were surprise visitors, they made us feel at home and comfortable. I used to love playing with the Moletsane children and their dogs until one day, out of the blue, one of the biggest dogs, called Columba, attacked me, taking a big chunk out of the back of my thigh. A year later, fully recovered but harbouring what would be a lifelong fear of big dogs, we moved to Gugulethu. This was in December 1985, and I can still remember the sheer joy of moving into our own home in NY 108. Given our claustrophobic living conditions over the previous year and three months, this house felt palatial to me.

Our comfortable three-bedroom house in Gugulethu was positioned towards the end of a road that led to a cemetery. My favourite thing about the house was that it shared a fence with the

Uluntu Community Centre. Here, at least once a week, movies were shown to a raucous crowd that filled the makeshift cinema to capacity. For a rural boy like myself, watching a movie was like a magical experience, which I spent the whole week looking forward to. We mostly watched Asian martial-arts movies that centred around kung fu action scenes. These blissful movie-watching experiences were often spoilt by stray rubber bullets fired by the police, supposedly directed at the toyi-toying mourners who marched past Uluntu Centre on their way to lay their loved ones to rest in the cemetery.

This back-and-forth aggression between mourners and police played out on NY 108 on an almost biweekly basis. A year later, after living and attending school in Gugulethu, I was accepted into St George's Grammar School, in Mowbray, where I would do my Standard 1 (Grade 3). Even though I would now be travelling in to the suburbs for school, my world was very much enveloped in township life. It was the time of consumer boycotts and neck-lacing. It was not uncommon to drive home from school to find a protest march that resulted in a burning truck tyre being placed around the neck of someone alleged to be a police collaborator. At other times we would witness people being stopped and forced to eat or drink cleaning products because they had bought their groceries from white-owned retail stores in defiance of the con-sumer boycott.

We could tell that tensions were building when, as kids, we were asked to participate in throwing stones at the police as they tried to keep order. Usually, the cost for those who partici-pated was having to duck rubber bullets and trying not to get tear-gassed. One Saturday in July 1987, a similar scene took place on the road where we lived, only this time the police were using live ammunition. By chance, we were not at home that day, as one of the bullets came through our roof. It was only when it rained that we noticed holes in the roof through which the water was leaking.

The last straw came one day shortly after that, when war broke out between the comrades and a faction known as the 'witdoeke', who were seen as collaborators with the security police. By midday our domestic worker had picked up a rumour that the warring parties were heading towards the Uluntu Centre, where some people were hiding. My mother was at work at UCT when she got a call from the domestic worker, who was in a state of panic. Mamphela drove like a madwoman to pick up my younger brother, Malusi, from the Uluntu crèche, pack a few essentials into the boot of the car and head to Rondebosch.

In her typical style, my mother dragged all of us to Francis Wilson's house and told him that we would be staying there with his family until we could find suitable accommodation at the university. Ironically, Francis and Mamphela had recently produced a report titled 'Children on the Front Line', documenting the cost of children participating as child soldiers or township anti-apartheid fighters. He was obviously willing to help us out of a situation – the dangers of which he knew all too well.

Based on 'Children on the Front Line', Mamphela began working as a full-time researcher at UCT. This would awaken in her a passion for social anthropology. From later that July 1987, we stayed in UCT staff housing on a street named Lovers Walk. Our house was located directly across from the UCT Ballet School, where I got the shock of my life seeing men in tights acting very effeminately. I learnt from this experience that men in big cities such as Cape Town clearly behaved in ways that might seem very peculiar to my nine-year-old self. As a family we took these changes in our stride, remaining close as a unit and keeping mostly to ourselves. My mother never let us forget that part of our core value system was respect for others and expectation of the reciprocation of that respect. My experience with the Ballet School taught me tolerance for what seemed like obvious differences between myself and others.

At this time, my mother reconnected with Father David Russell, who was ministering to migrant workers living in Langa, Gugulethu and Nyanga. These men, mostly from the eastern Cape, worked on the railways, in the port and in local factories. They were forced into low-level employment because this was all that was available; better jobs were protected by the so-called coloured labour preference policy, a form of apartheid influx control designed to favour coloureds over blacks. This reflected the reality that black people were viewed as 'serfs' in a feudal Cape economy that paid them as little as humanly possible. Mamphela's research into the plight of black migrant workers became the basis of her PhD thesis, titled 'The Politics of Space', which was later published in book form. This work put my mother in a position to observe the urban receiving end of the migrant labour system, compared to the source of migrant labour that she had observed in the rural environment surrounding Zanempilo.

In 1988 my mother's lawyer, Michael Richman, suggested that he could front for her to purchase a house for us in Mowbray, within walking distance of my school. When she shared this plan with the then vice-chancellor of UCT, Dr Stuart Saunders, he proposed that the university step in as the purchaser. This was a great relief for my mother and me. On more than one occasion I had been left at school to have supper with the boarders because she was stuck in a meeting and couldn't come to pick me up.

Each move that we made came with the typical childhood anxieties around switching neighbourhoods, making friends, losing friends, falling in love, losing love and all the while constantly adopting to new circumstances. Our moves sometimes took us to international destinations. I found myself living in Boston at two different times in my life. The first time was in 1988, when I was ten, and my mother went on a sabbatical as one of the first Mary Bunting Fellows at Harvard University. We stayed in Boston for six months. Though I could tell that my brother and I had stepped into an entirely different league in terms of the quality of education, I did not know until many years later that the school I attended, Buckingham Browne & Nichols School (BB&N), was considered one of the world's top schools.

I blossomed academically at BB&N, after being diagnosed there for the first time as being dyslexic. For many years I couldn't understand the disconnect between how quickly I grasped concepts in class and how poorly this understanding would translate come exam time. Teachers would always accuse me of sloppy work or say that I was not diligent in my application to my studies. What saved me from the worst effects of dyslexia was the fact that I was a keen reader from a very early age. The downside was that instead of failing, which would have drawn more attention to my disability, I just muddled through and achieved average marks.

Given my experience, I wonder how many black children have lived their lives with similarly undetected disabilities. It turned out that the two accommodations I needed were 15 minutes of extra time to complete maths exams and the ability to write essays on a computer that had spell-check. These two accommodations alone transformed my marks from average to As and Bs. When

I returned to St George's, I received very little help and my marks slipped back to run-of-the-mill.

Five years later, in 1993, my mother got a direct grant from the Carnegie Corporation of New York to do another sabbatical at Harvard University. Back in Boston, I achieved high marks and also excelled in several sports. When it came time to leave I was offered a scholarship to stay, but I declined it. I felt called to find my place within the context of my home, South Africa, so I could find a way to make my own contribution to its development.

As a child, I had no idea of the wide-reaching impact of my father's ideas and his legacy. I knew he was one of the foremost liberation leaders, but what that meant in the context of the big wide world was difficult for a 15-year-old to tell. Though it may be difficult for many people to remember, at that time the legacy of Steve Biko was muted in South Africa. In fact, Steve Biko was celebrated more internationally than in his own country. It was only when we went to live in Boston for the second time, from December 1993 to May 1994, that I first witnessed people's reaction to the Biko name and was made to understand the global nature of Steve Biko's legacy.

It was not a legacy that the apartheid government dared to talk about, and after 1994 a constituency within the ANC that did not want to share the credit for South Africa's liberation with the BCM made sure to de-emphasise my father's achievements. The most outrageous statement of ANC denial was the absence of references to Stephen Bantu Biko in Nelson Mandela's *Long Walk to Freedom*. When my mother confronted President Mandela about this omission, he was truly embarrassed, because it was an indication of his acquiescence to the small-mindedness of those in the ANC who had attempted to write my father out of history.

Steve Biko's legacy began to crystallise in my mind in 1989 when we visited Nelson Mandela in Victor Verster prison, outside Paarl. To the extent that I had any expectations at all, I had imagined him to be a very militant and scary person. Instead, I met a regal, grandfatherly figure who made me feel immediately at ease. Madiba told us how the political prisoners on Robben Island would read smuggled-in press clippings about my father. He spoke about how the prisoners admired what this 'young chap' was accomplishing in the early 1970s. He also let us know how deeply depressed and dismayed they were when they received the news of his death.

I was struck by the quiet serenity of the man, who spoke movingly of his admiration for my father. That Madiba looked up to Steve Biko as an embodiment of what a freedom fighter should be provided all the evidence I needed that my father's life had been well lived, and that his death was not in vain. In Madiba I was to have my first grandson/grandfather relationship. In retrospect, I am amazed that such a busy person found the time and the emotional space to be so available to me, and to so many others. In all of my greatest moments, be it a graduation, a wedding or a rite-of-passage ceremony, Madiba was always there. He always came physically, giving his financial and moral support where he could. The experience of being under his care transformed my life. It elevated the aspirations I had and motivated me to want to be great in all that I did.

Even as a teenager, I was acutely aware that the experiences afforded to me – to meet exceptional people, to travel, to receive a high-quality education – gave me an unusual amount of exposure to the wider world, which was a rare privilege. While I was born under trying circumstances, the exceptional good fortune I have enjoyed in terms of relationships, family support and exposure makes me believe that I was born at the right time.

There have always been good men who have stood in as surrogate father figures for me. They took me to my first live soccer games, came to support me during school sports, taught me how to ride a bike and helped me learn how to deal with conflict. These are the kinds of things that children from fatherless homes struggle with. Some of these tasks were performed by my elder brothers, Nkosinathi and Samora. Nkosinathi, who is seven years older than me, moved to Cape Town in 1990 after completing his post-matric at St Andrew's College in Grahamstown. He attended UCT, which meant I had daily contact with an older sibling for the first time.

One year later, my mother arranged for Samora, who is three years older than me, to enrol at St George's. At the same school together for the first time, Samora and I quickly became close. From my elder brothers, I learnt how to fight. I learnt how to respectfully disagree and to be respectful to my elders. They also taught me about social life, how to attract the attentions of the opposite sex and what was and was not cool. My mother provided a home environment for them in this foreign city. She did so out of her natural motherly instincts and her obligation to my father. While all of us were living in Cape Town, a tight bond enriched our lives. The timing for me was perfect. It was during this time that my identity as umXhosa male formed, allowing me the benefit of learning to follow my family's traditional customs.

For all three of us, and for my younger brother, Malusi, Uncle Malusi Mpumlwana has been a particularly important role model. We had different but equally close relationships with him, and I suspect we can all attest to his deft skill at being present in our lives without being overbearing. Few black boys have adult men in their lives with the kind of tolerance that Uncle Malusi displays.

He has always been there for us: when we got married, when there has been a death in the family or when we celebrated the birth of a child. He has done this both out of his intrinsic sense of decency as a human being and out of his deep sense of duty to our parents. His family has had to share him with us, and we are the richer for their generosity.

Two other men from my father's side have played a major role in our lives – Sekelezi (Seks) Duna and Solly (Sol) Duna, who are my father's first cousins on his mother's side. As young teenagers, Seks and Sol grew up in Mamcete's household and around the BCM, absorbing the philosophy as they spent countless hours with members of the leadership team.

In 1973, when my father received his banning order, Seks acted as his runner in Ginsberg. He would be sent out to buy cigarettes, beer and newspapers, to send messages to other members of the BCM and to facilitate illegal visits as necessary. Both he and Sol were too young to participate directly in the politics of the movement, so they were spared the long-term imprisonment or death that befell others.

Over the years, both Seks and Sol have contributed to our lives in all the different ways a father would be expected to. They are the first people we call when there is a joyful event in our lives and the first to call us at moments of pain. My father taught them how to be men because, like me, they grew up without fathers in their life.

From the first time I visited King William's Town and Ginsberg, I felt welcomed by everyone, but I felt most at home in Bra Seks's three-bedroom house. A gentle giant, Seks stands 1.94 metres in height, with broad shoulders and the biggest hands I have ever seen. When my father died, it was decided that he should take over the house my father had bought down the road from Mamcete's place. It was only fairly recently that I learnt he was living in the house where my parents would have raised me. Strangely, though, something about Bra Seks's house has always felt like a home away from home. Bra Seks and his wife, sis' Nontle, have over the years been very generous in creating a safe space for me in eQonce whenever it was needed.

For all these reasons, I consider myself extremely fortunate. In South Africa, in 2018, just under 38 per cent of all homes were not headed by a female. More than two-thirds of children are brought up without a father. This means there are 6.1 million homes without a father present. Many of these children have no positive role models. Less than 40 per cent of all families in South Africa have both parents. So-called broken homes are the norm rather than the exception in our country.

The situation on the ground is probably a lot worse than the statistics show. According to the World Health Organization, 31 per cent of South Africans consume alcohol, with 59 per cent of this group classified as binge drinkers.[36] More than 17 million South Africans are dealing with depression, substance abuse, anxiety, bipolar disorder or schizophrenia. This leaves the majority of children in this country living either in single-parent households or in homes where one of the parents is either an alcoholic or struggling with mental illness. Sadly, there are few systems or support structures in place to help these children.[37]

Studies have shown that one of the most important human development indicators is the form of support system a child has in their home. A child who is an integral part of a family structure feels a sense of belonging in the world that is essential for their socialisation. Both boys and girls who come from households without fathers display feelings of abandonment and anxiety, and often do not have the full range of normal emotional responses. Most importantly, children from such households lack a self-concept that is essential for self-esteem. As children, they do not feel precious, worthy or adored.

A combination of these factors has been shown to lead to low levels of assertiveness and self-respect. These factors make it difficult to achieve self-love. We should not be surprised, therefore, that South African children struggle at school, and that about half of the nearly one million children who enter the school system drop out and never complete matric. This has absolutely nothing to do with the mental capabilities of South African children. These children are alone in a learning experience that is meant to be accompanied by supportive adults. Sadly, their teachers are often not capable of being positive role models either. South Africa has not heeded Marcus Garvey's advice: 'Education is the medium by which a people are prepared for the creation of their own particular civilization, and the advancement and glory of their own race.'[38]

I believe another consequence of children growing up fatherless and with the economic challenges of single-income households is the prevalence of violent crime, including against women and children. To tackle some of the social ills we are faced with as a society, it would help to take heed of the theory of social change that the BCM managed to effect with the little resources it had available.

Families form the cornerstone of any society. In South Africa, the demographics dictate that the black family stands at the heart of society. South Africa needs a cultural revolution centred on the rebuilding of families and the restoration of self-love. Our cultural revolution needs to focus on the BCM's five pillars of self-reliance:

1. Teaching psychological liberation to all South Africans.
2. Reframing identities to transcend our historical legacy.
3. Anchoring our value system on African spiritual principles.
4. Cementing African culture as the default way of being in South Africa.
5. Inverting our economic development to become community-driven instead of top-down.

There are several individuals and institutions that have taken up the challenge by running with these five pillars. If we want to have a peaceful, functional society, the whole country needs to embrace these five time-tested solutions as supplements to current government policies.

11

Pale skin, white masks

When Steve Biko and his colleagues introduced the word 'black' as an adjective describing a new identity for indigenous South Africans, Cape Malays, coloureds and Indians, they set in motion the creation of a new, expansive psychological construct. Blackness was introduced as a natural foil to whiteness. In my father's mind, neither was a description based on skin colour.

In a leadership training session he led in 1971, he put it as follows: 'Being black is not a matter of pigmentation – being black is a reflection of a mental attitude. Merely describing yourself as black you have started on a road towards emancipation, you have committed yourself to fight against all forces that seek to use your blackness as a stamp that marks you out as a subservient being . . . Black people – real black people – are those who manage to hold their heads high in defiance rather than willingly surrender their souls to the white man.'[39]

In the 50 years since Steve Biko uttered those words, there has been a dramatic alteration of what the words 'white' and 'black' mean as reflections of South Africa's mental attitudes. As a result, we have to ask ourselves a key question: why does the word 'black' have such a drastically different meaning in the modern South

African context from the meaning given to it in 1971? We also have to re-examine what whiteness is as a mental attitude of a segment of the population living in today's South Africa.

To my mind, three broad developments have helped reconstitute blackness, making it virtually unrecognisable relative to its original conception. First, blackness was appropriated as a term by the ANC, UDF, PAC and Azapo to mean, in almost all cases, something different from what Steve Biko and the BCM meant it to be. The ANC has historically preferred the terms 'native' or 'African' as descriptors for indigenous South Africans. In the late 1970s and early 1980s it adopted the descriptor 'black Africans' to home in on Batwa/Bantu people and continued to use the adjectives 'coloured', 'Indian' and 'Malay' to describe other people 'of colour'. The PAC preferred the blanket term 'Africans' or 'indigenous people'. The UDF referred to blacks, coloureds, whites and Indians to describe members of the 'non-racial' society they wanted to help create. Of all of these organisations, Azapo was alone in remaining faithful to the original use of the term 'black' in its most expansive context.

Second, in 1994, the Interim Constitution enshrined a meaning of blackness that attempted to make the term a reference to pigmentation. Because the constitutional drafting process was dominated by the National Party, the ANC and the UDF, the use of the descriptors favoured by these three organisations became the officially accepted way to delineate between various 'racial groupings' in this country.

Third, after 1994, whiteness was allowed to exist as a descriptor that carried with it both the reference to pigmentation and the assumption of socio-economic superiority.

As a result of these three developments, one can no longer echo Steve Biko in saying that by 'merely describing yourself as black you have started on a road towards emancipation'. Given the BCM's pioneering of blackness as an ideological and political foil to whiteness, it is only right that we turn to Black Consciousness as a philosophy to make sense of what the future of both blackness and whiteness may be.

Many damning statistics can be quoted about South Africa's socio-economic reality, which will ring alarm bells for all who aspire to a stable, peaceful future for this country. As South Africans stare their biggest social problems in the face, most of its citizens cannot avoid assigning a skin colour to the face they see. Though there is a near-unanimous international consensus around the fact that the concept of race has no scientific basis, too many South Africans still cling to this concept for dear life. For many people, neither politics nor economics can be intelligently discussed without invoking race as exhibit A in their attempt to back up their arguments.

According to research published by the American Association for the Advancement of Science, DNA tests on ancient-European skeletons show that genes signifying pale skin only appeared within the past 8 000 years.[40] While this may seem like a long time, it begins to shrink when one considers that it represents just four per cent of the period that *Homo sapiens* has existed on this planet. The concept of whiteness is significantly newer. Though many an individual may have noticed that they were paler than another person, or the reverse, it was not until 1600 CE (Common Era) that 'whiteness as a class identity' was invented.[41] The purpose of inventing whiteness was to justify the enslavement of those who did not fit into this form of class identity.

It is easy to understand why this was such an attractive and indeed lucrative idea. It is also easy to understand why Europeans thought to use race to justify the desire to subjugate those indigenous people who were not as pale as they were. In 1652, when Jan van Riebeeck arrived at the Cape, he brought this idea with him as a weapon. What is impossible to understand is why this idea was kept alive after 1994, when South Africa became a democracy.

In retrospect, the pivotal mistake was made back in 1955, when the Freedom Charter was drafted. Two conflicting points were made by the framers of the Freedom Charter that set the country on the conceptual collision course we find ourselves on today. They wrote: 'South Africa belongs to all who live in it, black and white . . .' and '. . . that only a democratic state, based on the will of the people, can secure to all their birth-right without distinction of colour, race, sex or belief . . .' The first statement is in support of a multiracial South Africa, the second in support of a non-racial South Africa. The ANC insignia depicts a wheel whose four spokes represent each of the so-called racial groups framed by apartheid, a classification that is retained today.

The dilemma South Africa finds itself in can be summed up in one question: does South Africa aspire to multiracialism or non-racialism? Neville Alexander, on the one hand, understood non-racialism as follows: 'The acknowledgement of superficial differences should not become, even potentially, a lever for marginalisation or exclusion of any individual or group of people.'[42]

A multiracial nation, on the other hand, is a society made up of different racial groups. Anyone who has spent any time in South Africa, or reading about South Africa, would very quickly conclude that South Africans act, think, speak and fight like people in a multiracial society. Most people's analysis about what is wrong in society either starts or ends with racial undertones. South Africans are almost pathologically race-conscious. Yet Chapter 1 of the Constitution explicitly states that we are a non-racial society.[43]

Does this suggest that South Africa is too far gone down the track of a dysfunctional multiracial identity to sweep this race consciousness under the rug? Does consciousness of race make it impossible to deliver on the constitutional goal of a non-racial republic? I think that if he were alive today, Steve Biko would argue that this is not a question that should be posed to black South Africans.

As Anne Hope once insightfully observed, race is a problem introduced by those who deem themselves white. Whiteness as an identity needs to be slain before South Africa can hope to chart the path to non-racialism. Yet, as one would expect, asking the fox to diagnose the security shortfalls of the chicken coop is fraught with perilous consequences. Therefore, while the voluntary self-help dedicated to pale-skinned South Africans' unlearning racism is a critical undertaking, it has to be combined with the realisation that colour coding was brought with Jan van Riebeeck and should have become irrelevant with former president FW de Klerk. Based on their experience of the worst types of discrimination, indige-nous South Africans have to have an independent determination to enforce non-racialism through laws that are geared to erase racial categories and their accompanying pathologies.

Perhaps this realisation will force us to turn back to Steve Biko's analysis proposing the need for white South Africans to undergo a process of conscientisation before non-racialism can become a possibility. A first hint of this comes in *I Write What I Like*: 'I am not sneering at liberals and their involvement. Neither am I suggesting that they are the most to blame for the black man's plight . . . The liberal must fight for their own freedom and not that of the nebulous "they" with whom they can hardly claim identification.'[44] From this reading of Biko, an essential dilemma emerges. Can indigenous South Africans rely on those benefiting from white supremacy to voluntarily give up their wealth?

A close reading of his work suggests that the freedom Biko thought white people should fight for is freedom from their own oppression at the hands of a highly developed white superiority complex. Speaking at a student conference in 1971, Biko articulated this problem as follows: 'One has to overhaul the whole system in South Africa before hoping to get black and white walking hand in hand to oppose a common enemy. As it is, both black and white walk into a hastily organised integrated circle carrying with them the seeds of the destruction of that circle – their inferiority and superiority complexes.'[45]

We need to accept the fact that at a superficial level, the only colour differences we can observe are either darkness of skin colour or paleness of skin colour, with no inherent special properties outside of the regulation of our tolerance for the rays of the sun. We can therefore agree that while a pale skin may be objectively observed, it is only under the mask of the assumed white racial identity that we can rightly identify where the superiority complex is embedded.

In asking white people to fight for their own freedom, therefore, Biko was asking pale-skinned people to take off the mask of whiteness. Without the mask of whiteness we can begin to ask the logical question: what is the benefit of classifying people by the presence or absence of melanin in the induction of an individual's oxidative DNA base? It is clear that the benefits, if there are any, are trivial. Now that we are certain of the triviality of the race issue at an objective level, we can deal with the real issue at hand. What will it take for pale-skinned South Africans to remove their mask of whiteness?

In 2021 it is clear that the superiority complex that made people with pale skin believe they were ordained to rule over those not deemed white in South Africa no longer has any basis. It was only through the help of indigenous South Africans that, in 1994 and after, whiteness was let into our democracy by the back door. As a result, white superiority has been allowed to fester under the false pretence that in a materialistic post-apartheid South Africa, white European culture equals modernity. In modern South Africa, being *umlungu* signifies progress. In light of the hunger for material assets on the part of many indigenous South Africans, they have discarded the quest for true humanity in exchange for a quest to join the *umlungu* as a status group. Through their domination of media, advertising, publishing and the arts, people who regard themselves as whites have deliberately cultivated an image that those with pale skin and European mannerisms are cultured, intelligent, healthy, beautiful, rich and thus worth imitating.

It is easy to track the timeline from the point when indigenous South Africans aspired to be classified 'just' as ordinary South Africans to the point when some of them began to aspire to be treated as *umlungu*. In 1976, a year and a half before I was born, the ideology of the BCM so animated young black students that they rose up to resist the introduction of teaching in Afrikaans, imposed on them by the supposed superiority of white South African culture. Yet by the time I got to high school in 1990 the situation was completely reversed. Even though some of us came from homes where the slogan 'black power' was prominent, the reality of white supremacy was successfully seared into our minds. The black fists we saw on the ends of the combs we called 'Afro-picks' were but a drop of consciousness in an ocean of psychological repression.

Mentally, we had all but conceded our ability to fight the scourge of racism on every level we experienced it. We could fight about it once, maybe twice, a day, but every one of us engaged in some level of complicity, thereby helping to keep intact the white superiority complex. At school, we called our pale-skinned teachers 'sir'. On the farms where we worked, we called the pale-skinned farmer 'baas' and many of us, even as grown men, let him call us 'boys'. As women and men, while serving the pale-skinned lady in her home, we tripped over ourselves to call her 'madam'. In a factory, plant or retail business, if we worked for a young pale-skinned manager, we called him 'boss'. We are not talking about the 1960s or 1970s; what I describe are interactions that were the norm in 1990.

My father described the social cost of the asymmetric economic relationships between whites and blacks in the 1970s as follows: 'He cannot keep answering back to him every day: don't shout at me, don't swear at me, because there is also the element of the job he has to keep.'[46] Sadly, for many indigenous South Africans, this situation is still the norm today.

In the 15 years between my father's death and my enrolment in high school, apartheid basically beat indigenous South Africans into submission. After the BCM was dissolved, the teachings of Black Consciousness were mostly removed from the lexicon of the liberation struggle. This created a void in the black community, which was once again filled with self-doubt, self-hate and woundedness. Though the UDF fought vigorously to achieve freedom, its leaders gave much less thought to the psychological dimension of this freedom than the circumstances warranted.

My father and his BCM contemporaries understood that dehumanisation through legal means, spiritual means and the internalisation of demeaning ideas leads to self-hate. There is no more dangerous an idea than the acceptance of the false concept that white superiority is inevitable, except perhaps the belief that an indigenous South African can join the construct of whiteness as an attaché or *umlungu*.

Like the other constitutional goal of non-sexism, fighting for non-racialism cannot be done passively. Either we are explicitly calling out white superiority or we are implicitly condoning it. The charge of fighting against this backsliding into normalising white superiority has to be taken up primarily by pale-skinned South Africans, who should be morally compelled by right-thinking indigenous people to take off their white masks, so that we can walk together towards non-racialism.

I believe that indigenous South Africans are prevented from demanding that their pale-skinned fellow countrymen to take off their masks because of the entrenched socialised normalisation of white supremacy. The process of socialising the normalisation of white supremacy has always involved the use of fear. As Steve Biko explained: 'This interaction between fear and reaction then sets off a vicious cycle that multiplies both fear and reaction. This is what makes meaningful coalitions between black and white totally impossible.'[47]

Our biggest challenge as a country is that the status quo is propagated by an education system that teaches all of our children to accept white superiority as an ideal, not just a norm. Our private and public education systems both serve as vectors of this normalised brainwashing of indigenous children. It teaches them to bow to the white supremacist status quo through the history that they learn, which is chronologically tied to the ups and downs of so-called Western civilisation.

It subconsciously teaches children geography from the reference point of England and America, by designating some areas Middle East and others Far East. The South African school system reinforces the fact that African languages are not as important when it assigns lesser weight to indigenous languages than to English and Afrikaans in assessing the learner's overall score.

I am as guilty as many indigenous South Africans in allowing my children to be brainwashed in exchange for the privilege of attending one of South Africa's so-called top schools. Until we stop sending our children to these brainwashing centres of learning, or completely transform them, the future will look exactly like our past.

At many of these private schools, our children are in the minority and never represent more than a third of the class. Pale-skinned teachers are always in the majority, which deprives all the attending children of the opportunity to see indigenous figures of authority or role models as a social norm.

The history they are taught is focused on the European heritage of their pale-skinned classmates. The culture that dominates these schools is that of the Dutch and British forefathers of these pale-skinned students. The predominant language is English or Afrikaans. They cannot help but feel out of place in what is supposed to be an African society. In this way they are actively prepared for custodianship under a white superiority structure.

In her book *Conversations with My Sons and Daughters*, Mamphela Ramphele further emphasises this point: 'Affirmation of children's home culture builds self-confidence because it establishes equality alongside those from other cultures. They do not have to apologise for the fact that their name has clicks that the teacher is unable to pronounce, and so the child has to acquiesce to a nickname for the teacher's convenience . . .'[48] The themes she explores in this book should weigh heavily on all our minds as we make decisions about our children's schooling.

The African history that we accept our children learning at school still drips with condescension. The other day my son explained to me what he was taught about the Batwa people – the first inhabitants of South Africa. All the teacher had basically told them was that the Batwa were hunter-gatherers who knew where to find water in the desert. No attempt was made to connect him or anyone else in the class to these people. No aspect of modern life was ascribed to the Batwa. Even as they continued to learn that Bartolomeu Dias 'found the Cape of Good Hope', the Batwa people he found here were projected as having neither the rights nor the dignity necessary to designate them as owners of this land. No attempt was made to show and explain the many beautiful rock-art depictions of Batwa cosmology. No attempt was made to describe how the Batwa arrived at their understanding of God as Tixo. No explanation was given about how Batwa and Bantu people became what they are today.

Without this understanding being shared with both indigenous and pale-skinned South African children, the Batwa, the Bantu and other ancient-African people remain strangers in history to children who find themselves as strangers in modern times. Yet when they are told the 'heroic' stories of European colonisers, no stone is left unturned in positively contextualising their origins, their beliefs and motives, what drove their cultural preferences and what made them, in short, human.

So from very early on in the life of our children, we pay for the privilege of their being made to feel alien to their own people during the hours when they are at school. I am in a constant state of internal discord about the disservice I am doing my children by having them attend private schools. Yet as an economic investment in the future of my children, there are few better ways to ensure their success in life. They will almost certainly be better equipped than children who go to public schools to join corporate South Africa, where the culture often mimics that of private schools such as Michaelhouse, Bishops, Herschel or Hilton. To put an end to these moral dilemmas, we have to transform the quality of our public-education system. Simultaneously, the teaching and learning culture of both public and private education has to be completely overhauled.

Every generation that the current education system is allowed to influence sets us back ten to fifteen years. This is because the privileged, pale-skinned young South Africans who attend these private schools inherit their social privilege from their parents. They in turn stand guard over the inherited social codes that restrict the rest of South Africans from 'unwarranted entry'. Their role as future leaders of these institutions ensures that the status quo is retained.

This status quo has been entrenched by constitutional rights that allow certain freedoms, including those that protect pale-skinned South Africans from scrutiny of their superiority complex and the elitism that maintains it. As a result, white supremacists are secure in the fact that no one can rob them of their right to pass down their privilege. They are able to claim freedom of speech if they want to defend white superiority, or rely on the protected right to vote for a local government solely constituted to defend their narrow white-supremacist interests. All the while, the mask they assume allows them the right to look down on corrupt government officials and criminal black elements in their neighbourhood. Surely this is a path to a dysfunctional form of multiracialism that can only result in a popular uprising?

In April 2021 former President Thabo Mbeki took to social media to ask the following important but rhetorical question: 'We must surely be living in a very strange country. This week, Statistics South Africa released a report which apparently shows that black Africans aged between 25 and 34 are less skilled than their parents. Why is there no national outcry – a focused discussion about what we must do to attend to this national emergency?'

I can imagine, given how highly most of us regard our former president, there will be a vigorous discussion about why this is the case. I am certain most will use a materialist explanation to arrive at an answer. To me, however, the answer is embedded in the question. That Statistics South Africa still has to separately track a segment of our population it refers to as 'black African' may point to the heart of the issue. These 'black Africans' may have come to the rational conclusion that their education, in a country that regards them as a relic of the past, may not be as useful in their future acquisition of economic opportunities, because the thumb on the economic scales tips all things in favour of the maintenance of white supremacy.

Steve Biko might as well have been writing of South Africa in 2021 when he described this form of institutionalised racism: 'The racism we meet does not only exist on an individual basis; it is also institutionalised to make it look like the South African way of life. Although of late there has been a feeble attempt to gloss over the overt racist elements in the system, it is still true that the system derives its nourishment from the existence of anti-black attitudes in society. To make the lie live even longer, blacks have to be denied a chance of accidentally proving their equality with white men. For this reason there is job reservation, lack of training in skilled work and a tight orbit around the professional possibilities for blacks.'[49]

Today, the lie of white superiority is still clung to by too many indigenous South Africans in power, who seek to rule through the legitimacy bestowed on them by pale-skinned businesspeople. This lie is maintained by corporate South Africa through the manipulation of the latent inferiority complex of many of the indigenous government officials appointed to regulate their business activities. It is also maintained by pale-skinned teachers who deliberately show bias towards pale-skinned children in class or on the sports field, allowing them to prosper further. This same lie is perpetuated by many of us parents who pay for our children's cultural brainwashing. We are all complicit in keeping this lie alive.

Fortunately, young people continue to prove that a little bit of truth goes a long way. In March 2015 a group of UCT students threw faeces at a bronze statue of Cecil John Rhodes, one of the world's most corrupt and brutal colonialists, that stood on their campus. The statue was seen as a symbol of the unchanging colonial mindset still held by many at the university.

With this act of defiance, the movement that would become known as #RhodesMustFall was born. The movement drew students on most university campuses around South Africa, who revolted against the continued nonchalant display of symbols of oppression at institutions of higher learning. By calling for the decolonisation of university campuses, these students refused to acknowledge the 'European roots' of these educational institutions, which white supremacists so casually highlight, as symbols of a proud history.

In a recent interview, Chumani Maxwele, the first student to throw faeces on the Rhodes statue at UCT, recalled what drove him to this act. He said he chose 9 March 2015 to collect human waste from the Cape Town township of Khayelitsha because it coincided with an annual public art festival called Infecting the City. For Maxwele, the symbolism was about reclaiming public spaces for the public. In an ironic twist, Infecting the City is curated by UCT's Institute for Creative Arts.

Like other major South African institutions and organisations, UCT has preoccupied itself with surviving the attempts made by various vice-chancellors to transform the institution. Having lived on and around the UCT campus for over ten years (my mother was deputy vice-chancellor of UCT from 1991 to 1996 and vice-chancellor from 1996 to 2000), I can attest to the attitudes held by many professors, administrators and alumni. According to them, UCT was a centre of excellence *despite* transformation, not because of it. For those who held this view, the sooner black people could grasp what a gem they had inherited, the sooner we could work together to thwart efforts to destroy the great traditions of the university. Uncle Barney had similar experiences while he was the vice-chancellor of Unisa; the prospect of a change to the status quo was vigorously fought by the white-supremacist establishment.

This same attitude towards transformation also permeates corporate South Africa, the civil service, town-planning offices and the Department of Arts and Culture, to name just a few. Faced with the charge of transforming these institutions, those at the top are met with a Berlin Wall-like resistance. In Biko's own words: 'So as a prelude whites must be made to realise that they are only human, not superior. Same with blacks. They must be made to realise that they are also human, not inferior.'[50]

Steve Biko was an absolutist about freedom. Either freedom must be shared equally by all or it should not be had by anyone.

This was Biko's intense consciousness of what freedom really meant. One of his intellectual influences, the philosopher Hegel, is famous for saying that 'the history of the world is none other than the progress of the consciousness of freedom'. Young people like Chumani Maxwele have taken on board this absolutist understanding of freedom. Many more like him from the #RhodesMustFall and #FeesMustFall movements are privately seething at being forced to endure white supremacism in the workplace. Their consciousness of freedom will not allow them to let things stand for much longer. Should we wait for them to throw faeces at white-supremacist power structures or should we be more proactive?

There are many young political actors who have taken up the rhetorical baton from the BCM to express their intimate consciousness of freedom. The likes of Julius Malema, Floyd Shivambu, Mbuyiseni Ndlozi, Zolile Xalisa and Andile Mngxitama have all articulated a full-frontal attack on white supremacy. Where some of them have failed is in meeting the exacting moral standard asked of indigenous freedom fighters who seek to take on the system. Negative aspects of their past or missteps made in their political lives have been brought up to rubbish the substance of the points they are making.

As a result of our constitutional democracy, the South African media has been given the right to determine who is a credible carrier of public messages, particularly those messages that seek to unseat existing power structures. The media has seen to it, in its wisdom, that only politically moderate indigenous voices dominate the airwaves, leading to a softening of the critique of modern white supremacy.

Without credible voices to pick up the BCM mantle in South Africa's public discourse, the entrenchment of iniquitous, race-based, economic distribution of wealth will go unchecked. History has proven that the challenge Steve Biko was attempting to take on was more intricate than anyone could have guessed. The BCM adherents dedicated themselves to affirming the humanity of black people.

This same humanity is used against indigenous people by those within the white community who continue to hold on to their white-supremacist identity. They have chosen to weaponise ubuntu against indigenous people by taking advantage of the general population's inclination to forgive and seek common ground.

In words that echo Steve Biko, the philosopher and theologian Paul Tillich once wrote that 'the courage to be is the ethical act in which man affirms his being in spite of those elements of his existence which conflict with his essential affirmation'.[51] Instead of pale-skinned South Africans finding in themselves the burning need to feel superior by using whiteness as part of their affirmation of self, perhaps they could find the courage in Tillich's words, to satisfy themselves of their equality with indigenous South Africans.

Many of my pale-skinned friends ask me why they are, many years after the fact, still associated with white colonialism. The simple answer lies in the definition of 'colonise', which is to settle and establish control over the indigenous people of an area. In every way possible, white supremacists in South Africa have colonised and continue to colonise this country. They did this initially through military repression, then through the genocide that was the apartheid system, and lately through psychological control in post-apartheid South Africa. This psychological control has been maintained in two broad forms: first, through *control over the aspirations* of indigenous people, and, second, through the conditioning of indigenous people through the *power of low expectations*. Let us unpack these two notions in more detail.

Controlling indigenous aspirations

Indigenous people have been conditioned to want all things that would cloak them in the trappings of white supremacy and its accompanying label of modernity. The clothes we wear, the cars we drive, the food we eat and all the trappings of 'modern life' are part of a larger institutionalised process of social conditioning. As human beings who live in a capitalist society, we are reduced by the system to becoming the sum total of our aspirations. An indigenous person who publicly enjoys rare and exotic material things is seen to have 'made it'. There is no doubt that many of these trappings of modern life are associated with white superiority, with little or no scrutiny as to whether white supremacists even had anything to do with their creation. A good example is the tendency to describe all science and technology as 'Western' and therefore white. Even if Asians, Arabs, Africans or South Americans made these products, the common refrain to any progressive invention is to lump it under the misnomer 'Western technology'.

Collectively, we have reached a point where it has become impossible to distinguish what South Africans think of as modern and aspirant from the interests of what the white institutional structure deems necessary to retain white supremacy. This is because of the accommodation we make to white supremacy as individuals. Things that are locally made are implicitly deemed undesirable. Supporting businesses that are indigenous is only cool if not too many other indigenous people patronise the business. The very nature of what looks 'cool' is wrapped up in the clutches of white supremacy.

Apart from indigenous people's lust for foreign-made products and gadgets, our national aspiration to sovereignty has been rendered mute. As a nation, we have officially completed the self-fulfilling prophecy that to be trusted in the modern world, our leaders have to indicate that our country adheres to global rules. Critical to this assurance to abide by these rules is to ensure that those bodies appointed to score our performance in protecting the interests of white supremacists, such as global credit-rating agencies, are not only free to do so but also feel comfortable travelling and doing business in our country. The lack of experience to credibly give these assurances and competently see to their successful outcomes has led to the belief that it is best that pale-skinned people show indigenous people how. They do this by running the organisations that matter in South Africa. If these assurances are met, then we are told that we will get foreign direct investment.

However, there is a catch: in order for foreign direct investment to be long term in nature, the world would like to know that we will never forcibly remove the pale-skinned people with whom they are accustomed to doing business. In short, retaining the status quo will ensure that we are judged to be running a fiscally and politically sound country. This is driven home by the oft-trumpeted fact that our economy only has a few corporate and individual taxpayers, and therefore we should listen to their concerns about the way the fiscus spends their money.

This unspoken, well-entrenched, self-fulfilling prophecy is the subtext of most financial articles, news reports, business-lunch topics and many of the economic analyses published in financial magazines. It is a not-so-subtle weapon of compliance. This self-fulfilling prophecy is, in short, the basis for the sustained use of pale-skinned people's white masks to control native behaviour.

Fiscal and political responsibility has yet to be redefined in a context of a developing economy that has unsustainable inequality. Yet, as bitterly as they sometimes complain about this state of affairs, most of our government officials do as they are told. Even some of our indigenous intelligentsia spill plenty of ink in the media to underscore the perils that await us if we do not listen to this prophecy.

This is, of course, not a new form of engagement between colonialists and indigenous people. Uncle Malusi Mpumlwana once explained to me that the term amaXhosa people use to denote a backward or rural person, *iqaba*, was actually a reference to Pondo people who defied missionaries in 1834 by putting on their traditional regalia and the skin paint that went with it, as opposed to wearing European clothes, as many amaXhosa people who had converted to Christianity did. Modern South Africans are caught in this same type of Morton's fork, or false dilemma: comply with the status quo or be relegated as an *iqaba*.

The power of low expectations

A second psychological mechanism that holds indigenous people back is the tendency, identified by Paulo Freire, for oppressed people to carry a deadly fear of freedom. Freire understood that to release the oppressed from their way of being is not as easy as removing the forces of oppression. The voting patterns of South Africans, their rate of patronising businesses owned by white monopoly capital and the large percentage of government business that goes to white-owned corporations are public displays of a very strong fear of freedom.

The government has a great influence over the South African economy. If our government officials were not scared to be free,

South Africa could have its sovereignty back. Instead, white supremacy has successfully taught indigenous South Africans to lower their expectations of the future and be happy when they receive a fraction of even these lowered expectations. After repeating this cycle for years, indigenous people have become conditioned to ill-treatment. So much so that we find it difficult to distinguish between behaviour designed to placate our anger, behaviour designed to divide us from other indigenous people, behaviour designed to make us feel grateful for the little we have and behaviour designed to remind us of our 'real place' in society.

Doing this seems to be second nature for white supremacists who play this deft game of indigenous South African expectation management. They therefore conveniently fail to recognise how they manipulate those whom they seek to control into a particular mindset that serves their agenda at that time. This mindset has allowed a pale-skinned minority to shape how the majority of South Africans adjust to their presence. It is only due to low expectations of ourselves that indigenous people allow our target to be the 25 per cent ownership of our economy, even though we are over 80 per cent of the population. It is also as a result of low expectations that we have a situation where the indigenous intelligentsia makes a serious attempt to apologise for, and to critique, the system of welfare benefits for poor South Africans when these do not add up to more than R2 000 on average per individual per month.

The same low expectations allow many of us to be satisfied with the status quo in corporate South Africa, where more than 65 per cent of all managers are pale-skinned.[52] Because of low expectations, we can accept the glib explanation that indigenous people have yet to build the skills and expertise to run their own economy. This leads to an economy run by a type of discriminatory discernment characterised by white-supremacist management selling goods and services to indigenous customers while fastidiously avoiding investing in indigenous entrepreneurs.

According to a recent report in *Business Insider SA*, the top 20 executives in South Africa collectively own more than R280 billion worth of shares on the Johannesburg Stock Exchange. Only five of these 20 executives are not pale-skinned. This is against the backdrop of 16.5 million people (almost exclusively indigenous) collectively receiving R259 billion in social grants. The wealthiest 15 pale-skinned people in South Africa have more resources at their disposal than more than 16 million indigenous people!

This modern form of colonialism is cultural, psychological and normative, all without leaving the fingerprints of white-supremacist dominance on the dominated indigenous people. Instead of a victimless crime, this is in fact a perpetrator-less crime. Many of the pale-skinned people I know would swear that they do not participate in anything of this nature. Those wise enough to recognise what they are doing believe it is a reflexive reaction that they cannot stop, any more than they can stop breathing.

Whether a South African is rich, poor, powerful, well-travelled or an *iqaba*, this evolved form of colonialism currently roots us to the spot. This perpetrator-less crime leaves only the superiority complex among pale-skinned people and a growing inferiority complex among the indigenous colonised masses as evidence of its existence.

Pale-skinned people feel comfortable in the new South Africa as long as the focal point of any transformation effort does not force them to confront their own dehumanisation. Though Black Consciousness was developed precisely to deal with this very specific form of dehumanisation, its premature death in the late

1970s meant that its mission was not complete. As a result, many members of other political formations fail to understand the magnitude of the challenge posed by white superiority.

This lack of vigilance regarding the scourge of white supremacy allows many pale-skinned South Africans to adopt a form of citizenship that goes with an optional participation right in our society. It is bad enough that many middle- and upper-class pale-skinned South Africans have dual passports, which reflects this optional attitude to their citizenship. What is worse is that they seek to condition everyone they deal with to publicly acknowledge their ability to take their labour anywhere in the world if they are not shown the appropriate gratitude for their contributions to this country. This is unheard of anywhere else in the world.

Steve Biko warned us that even when we are politically free, the biggest threat to this country would be what he called 'white souls in black skins' who would slow down liberation by promoting gradualism under white trusteeship. These white souls in black skins have found their soul mates in the pale-skinned South Africans who wear white masks. Together they perpetuate gradualism as a norm through the control of indigenous people's aspirations and the management of indigenous people's expectations.

Under these conditions, how can South Africans hope to bring to life a non-racial society? In the face of such psychological oppression, how can we aspire to be compassionate, sympathetic or generous in our behaviour? In a war with white supremacy, how can we continue to hold on to the values of ubuntu?

There are no simple answers to these questions. The only real answer is that we have to implement a national programme to break free from white-supremacist control over the aspirations of indigenous people and free indigenous people from the power of low expectations. This cannot be achieved until South Africa calls out those pale-skinned people who want to be a long-term part of a truly free South Africa, and insists that they adhere to the values of ubuntu by dropping their white masks – or face the consequences. The consequences the country creates, for what should be considered a national enemy, have to be grave enough such that the battle lines are clear. Anything that is a public good should not be available to white supremacists seeking to subvert non-racialism.

This, of course, will not happen for as long as South African voters cling to their fear of freedom. Only voters with a phobia of freedom will continue to complain about the poor quality of their leadership, as if someone else voted them in. Only voters with a fear of freedom would let their leaders cow them into retaining a constitution that has economic provisions specifically intended to maintain the status quo.

South Africa has to face one of its biggest crises head-on. Contrary to public belief, the biggest crisis is not corruption, entitlement, abuse of power or even poverty (even though these challenges have to be tackled urgently). It is the scourge of dehumanisation that is a result of pale-skinned South Africans who cling to their superiority complex. What are we to make of indigenous South Africans' sheepish adherence to the status quo?

To my father, the theory that black people can work within the system that seeks to oppress them is evidence of a lack of self-belief, and an acceptance that whites are the only South Africans who have the answers. Forty-four years after Biko's death, black people have little to show for their gradualist efforts. As much as the ANC, as a party, has built a world-class competence in mass mobilisation, the softly-softly approach to change management taken by the ANC government has failed to dislodge white supremacy. In fact, under the ANC government that many of us support, the status quo has been maintained so devotedly that indigenous people are now in charge of their own oppression.

This has only happened because we have ignored Steve Biko's warning about the importance of aligning both the means and goals of our resistance to the system to attain total liberation. Before we can hope to attain the lofty goals of radical economic transformation or economic freedom for all, indigenous people have to deal with our inability to assert ourselves in the management of our own country.

This inability to be consistently assertive is one of the greatest challenges of my generation. As those of us in our thirties, forties and fifties assume leadership responsibilities, we cannot make the same mistake of gradualism made by those leaders immediately before us. In all of our various jobs, we are confronted with the choice of submitting to the system that tries to make us conform to norms set by those seeking to preserve the existing order or asserting our whole selves to change the situation. We make this choice many times a day, at work or in our communities. On those days when we convince ourselves to submit to the system, we return home a little bit more emotionally beaten down.

On those days when we choose to stand up for ourselves and assert our humanity, we find our spirit strengthens, our backs stiffen with pride and we are able to return home as whole versions of ourselves. This applies to people bagging groceries, running government departments, sweeping floors, driving taxis or working in big companies. The need to bring our whole self to work, and to reject a gradualist approach to unveiling who we are and what we want to achieve, is greater than ever. Like anything else in life, it becomes a force of habit and creates its own momentum governing our future behaviour.

In rejecting a gradualist approach, we have to find ways of co-opting and convincing many well-meaning South Africans who happen to have pale skins to drop their white masks and join us in assuming an identity as ordinary South Africans working together to build a non-racial society. Those who refuse to embrace non-racialism have to be fought as any people breaking our constitutional principles should, through any legal means necessary, to disabuse them of the notion that anyone in 2021 will be allowed to hide behind a white mask.

12

The BCM within the ANC

On a clear, crisp spring day in 2012, my mother and I went for a walk on the Sea Point Promenade to discuss something that had been on her mind for a long time. Back then I was living in Johannesburg, but I was in Cape Town that day on business. I had learnt to relish any opportunity to talk things through with her, as she has much wisdom to share and brings a helpful sense of clarity to decisions both big and small.

The backdrop to our discussion was a country in full-blown crisis. President Jacob Zuma and his allies had dug in their heels around the Nkandla scandal and denied that government money had been illegally used to finance the improvements to the president's homestead. Construction on the project had begun in 2009, and by the time it was complete, more than R240 million had been spent. Though President Zuma was loved by ordinary South Africans, the Nkandla scandal was just one of the many missteps in the Zuma administration's track record.

At that time, few of my mother's friends in the ANC were prepared to take a definitive stance on this and other very obvious signs of corruption and maladministration. That day, I could see that my mother's blood was boiling.

She couldn't believe that South Africans were letting one person run the country with such impunity. She mentioned over and over again that this was not what she and her fellow activists had fought for. I told her that many in my generation felt they were not senior enough to stand up to the impunity being displayed by the ANC at the time.

About a year later in 2013, the South African public would become aware of the intimate relationship that existed between Zuma and the Gupta family. A private jet chartered by the Guptas, carrying guests for a glittering family wedding to be held at Sun City, was permitted to land at Waterkloof Air Force Base, in Pretoria. The unprecedented landing of a private aircraft at a military base had been authorised at the highest level, and helped reveal the extent of the Gupta family's influence on government business. Despite the ensuing scandal, opinion polls indicated that Zuma would easily win re-election in the 2014 general election. A large part of the reason why was that many indigenous South Africans, especially those of us over 35, would only trust the ANC with our vote. A handful of parties had launched new platforms only to turn out to be a flash in the pan. No political party that focused on winning the votes of indigenous people had, at that time, created a formula for successful, sustained opposition.

That day in early 2012, when my mother and I went for a walk, she was considering three options: to retain her role as a public intellectual, to join the Democratic Alliance (DA) and lead that party into the next election, or to start her own political platform. We discussed the pros and cons of each option and assessed how ready ordinary South Africans were for change. I could tell she wanted to be involved in a hands-on manner. She felt hypocritical sitting in her nice house, writing articles about the change that was needed. Despite her many years of service to the nation, she seemed up for a final tour of duty. The question in her mind ultimately boiled down to going it alone or going with the DA.

Instinctively, we both felt uncomfortable with the politics of the DA, as they seemed to be running a campaign that was anti anything that was part of the indigenous South African agenda. While the DA was apparently trying to give young politicians opportunities to lead – a process former DA leader Tony Leon would later describe as 'an experiment gone wrong'[53] – we both thought that her joining them would be a bad idea.

At that time the DA was led by Helen Zille, whom my mother had known for many years. Helen had gained fame as a journalist in the late 1970s when she exposed the cover-up surrounding my father's death in detention. Later, she had served as UCT's executive director of communications during Mamphela's tenure as vice-chancellor of the university. The two women had developed a strong rapport and had several close friends in common.

Helen used all avenues available to her to woo my mother into becoming the new leader of the DA, but Mamphela decided she did not want to trumpet a DA agenda, which she felt was very much at odds with her core political beliefs. With that decision made, there was only one remaining direction to take: Mamphela would start a new party. AgangSA was founded in mid-February 2013.

Looking from the outside, what I really admired about the way my mother went about things with AgangSA was that she did not at any point consume herself with discussions about positions or allow her own ambitions to drive the agenda. She immediately empowered younger people to run with individual tasks and took on what they couldn't do. Even if it took several election cycles to make a major impact, she seemed resigned to a slow and steady build-up of the new political platform.

In December 2013 the news came that Nelson Mandela had passed away. My mother and I attended the memorial service in Pretoria together. As we got off a bus for dignitaries, we bumped into Helen Zille, who said something to the effect that it was time that she and my mother talked. My mother hadn't noticed her communication, so I passed on the message, but since I was extremely busy at work, several weeks went by and I forgot all about the interaction with Helen.

One day I found my mother at my house in Johannesburg, hurriedly getting ready for a meeting. I could tell that she was tired, and the pressure she was feeling from all sides was starting to show. Madiba's funeral had reminded her that imperfect unions are sometimes the handmaidens of seismic change. This is particularly true in politics.

As a way of honouring a man who had been her mentor and friend for close to three decades, she had convinced herself that now was the time to merge AgangSA with the DA. For her, the overwhelming reason to make this move was to achieve the greatest good for the most South Africans. She could not see segregated opposition parties defeating the ANC, hence it became clear to her that an aggregation of the political opposition was the best way forward. In the previous weeks she and Helen had had intense discussions on how such a merger would work.

That day when I met her at my house was a few days after the announcement had been made that the merger would take place. After the announcement, Helen yielded to pressure inside her party to avoid a reverse take-over by the smaller AgangSA. She began sending signals through the media that the first step was for my mother to join her party and that the rest would be discussed at a later date. At that point it became clear that my mother was going to be put in a corner and forced to leave the rest of her senior AgangSA leadership team behind.

On her way to the car that was to take her to the meeting, my mother and I had a hurried discussion during which I shared my honest opinion that she had no leverage in these negotiations. Her best strategic course of action would be to join the DA, become party leader and then push for the type of integration she was seeking with AgangSA. From the look on her face, I realised that what I had said offended every fibre in her body. From her point of view, a deal was a deal and Helen could not be allowed to get away with betraying her at this early stage. This had clearly become a values-based decision.

I felt a deep sense of sadness that things had come to this. We both knew that she would be attacked from both sides of the political divide if she refused to sign on the dotted line. I couldn't believe that after all of her sacrifices during her last tour of political duty, she was forced to commit political suicide because of her principled opposition to leaving behind the people she had started AgangSA with. To her, such a move was tantamount to selling out. We looked at each other and said nothing further. In that moment my admiration for her bravery jumped several notches. Out she went, got into the back seat of the waiting car and was driven away. The rest, as they say, is history.

Mamphela Ramphele joined the ranks of men and women such as Phumzile Mlambo-Ngcuka (former deputy president), Terror Lekota (former minister of defence), Mbhazima Shilowa (former Gauteng premier), Bishop Mvume Dandala, Bantu Holomisa (leader of the United Democratic Movement) and Patricia de Lille (minister and party leader) – all politically active citizens who were forced into the political wilderness due to their principled stance against one of the two big political parties.

Though many of her friends and former BCM colleagues joined the ANC, for my mother this was never an option. Mamphela had a long-standing issue with the culture of the governing party, which she thought perpetuated a command-and-control form of governance that forced its supporters to fall in line with bad decisions. She hated the fact that in the ANC, meritocracy had become a four-letter word. Most of all, she couldn't stand what the ANC had done to many of her BCM comrades. She felt they had been politically used, philosophically ignored by the decision-making structures of the ANC and morally compromised by having to recant their core political values.

To understand her concerns, one has to appreciate the history of former BCM members within the ANC. As I have previously described, although my father was the driving force of the BCM, he was supported by many talented and devoted people. With the founding of the BCM, talent naturally gravitated towards this vanguard youth movement because the issues they were raising so clearly spoke to the socio-economic condition of the average South African. Initially, the movement consisted of students who were members of SASO. The addition of more programmes, publications and political initiatives soon attracted a broader audience.

As the students grew older or graduated, a decision had to be made about what organisational body older members should belong to. One of the turning points in the development of the BCM came in mid-1972 with the formation of the BPC. A spirited series of debates took place between members of two conflicting schools of thought within the BCM. One of these was championed by Kenneth Hlaku Rachidi, who argued that young revolutionaries all over the world were turning their ideas into action through the creation of political platforms that could directly challenge authority. Thus, they should all join the armed struggle.

Steve Biko represented the contrary view, which was that the BCM had always been a cultural movement aimed at psychological liberation and was meant to serve as a moral leader in society without engaging directly in party politics. My father's belief was that when the time was right, this posture would allow the BCM to be a facilitator of the different political formations both in exile and underground.

My father lost this debate, but he followed the will of the movement's members in implementing the resolution to create an umbrella organisation, under which all BCM structures would operate. An inevitable consequence of the creation of the BPC was that its entire leadership immediately found themselves in the crosshairs of the apartheid state's security machinery.

On 26 February 1973 Biko, Barney Pityana, Harry Nengwenkulu and five other leaders of the BCM were banned for five years while actively running leadership-development workshops all over the country. These workshops were part of a deliberate attempt to decentralise the movement's knowledge base and set the tone for its leadership style. Teaching leaders how to lead while following the guiding principles of Black Consciousness was a mantra of the organisation.

The banning order required all of them to return to their hometowns. The apartheid police believed that immobilising the leadership of the BCM would bring an end to the movement. In 1974 the government passed the Affected Organisations Act, which prohibited foreign donors from funding groups such as the BCM and any of its affiliated organisations. Though many of the original leadership group remained active, further widespread arrests followed later in 1974 when they organised the pro-Frelimo rallies.

Little did the government know that through these arrests, they were laying the groundwork for the BCM leadership to be recruited by, and eventually migrate to, the ANC. The ANC deployed a network of operatives in neighbouring states, such as Lesotho, Botswana, Zimbabwe, Zambia and Mozambique, charged with facilitating the exile of BCM members, and successfully converting them to the ANC. Former president Thabo Mbeki personally oversaw this effort.

One example of this diffusion of talent from the BCM to the ANC is Nkosazana Dlamini-Zuma, currently minister of cooperative governance and traditional affairs. She obtained her BSc degree in zoology and botany from the University of Zululand, and then enrolled to study medicine at the University of Natal. During this time, she joined SASO and rose through the ranks to become vice president in 1975. After suffering harassment from the security police, she was forced to go into exile. Dlamini-Zuma made her way to London, where she served as head of the ANC Youth Section in Britain while continuing her studies at the University of Bristol, from where she graduated in 1978 as a medical doctor.

Along with Dlamini-Zuma, the younger generation of SASO leaders included the likes of Mathews Phosa, Terror Lekota, Cyril Ramaphosa, Makhenkesi Stofile, Aaron Motsoaledi and Joe Phaahla. They started to assume positions of leadership when the first generation of BCM leaders were arrested, banned or killed. While circumstances did not allow for all of them to be fully trained in the BCM philosophy and methods, this new leadership group gained enough understanding of what true liberation entailed to dedicate their lives to the struggle for the emancipation of South Africans.

Because of this diffusion of talent from the BCM to the ANC, some BCM beliefs also migrated to the ANC with the leaders who joined the liberation movement, creating some similarities in their objectives and approaches to the freedom struggle. As a result, there are many things the ANC and the BCM agree about. Each organisation believed that its leaders should lead their movement in its mission to organise and inspire the masses such that they become their own liberators. The BCM and the ANC both publicly strove for the creation of a united, non-racial, non-sexist and democratic society, and both organisations have called for the pursuit of fundamental change to create a better life for all, albeit at different times in history. Both defined this 'better life' as one that seeks the equitable distribution of political, social and economic opportunities among all South Africans.

For all the similarities in terms of their objectives, each organisation used very different tools of analysis to assess how to prioritise their objectives. These different tools of analysis led to a fundamental divergence in the theory of how change happens.

The BCM always prioritised cultural-change agency as both the means to an end and an end in itself. This theory of change was informed by the following quotation from Paulo Freire: 'Dehumanisation, which marks not only those whose humanity has been stolen, but also (though in a different way) those who have stolen it, is a distortion of the vocation of becoming more fully human.'[54] Steve Biko captured this sentiment when he said that the profound obligation of any African freedom fighter was to find a way to show the world a more human face.[55]

Given this framework of analysis, change would only come when the goal of liberating black people and their oppressors was met. This theory of change operates within a framework of analysis that was influenced by Hegel. As I have mentioned before, the BCM leaders believed that, at a fundamental level, everything is connected and participates in a lifelong dynamic evolutionary cycle.

To the extent that we are dealing with the identity of things, people or ideas, the BCM shared Hegel's famous concept of grouping phenomena into three related concepts – thesis, antithesis and synthesis. Everything progresses through these three stages. Indeed, the progression of things through these three stages is what Hegel defined as history.

Working from this framework, the BCM identified the concept of blackness as something that needed to be positively described in the form of a thesis. They did so by describing blackness as beautiful, powerful, virtuous and a source of pride. The antithesis to this was the white oppressive forces in this country, which the BCM defined as corrupt, immoral, bullying and lacking legitimacy and virtue.

The synthesis was that to be black is about recognising and taking pride in one's beauty, power and virtue. This recognition forces one to act in opposition to what is corrupt, immoral and illegitimate. Therefore, black people's opposition to white oppression was the ultimate assertion of their humanity over an inhumane state of affairs.

According to Barney Pityana, the philosophical underpinnings of the BCM were routinely mocked by staunch ANC members as representing an almost childlike analysis of politics. The ANC's theory of change was one of negotiation, armed struggle, mass mobilisation and international pressure in the form of sanctions. These four methodologies were enacted simultaneously. At its core, this framework of change is a numbers game. The more military capability the ANC acquired, the larger its threat and capacity to inflict terror on South Africa's white population. This threat was primarily used to force the governing National Party to the negotiating table. Similarly, the more people mobilised to make certain parts of South Africa ungovernable, the quicker the National Party would begin negotiations. The same thinking applied to the pressure brought to bear on the white-minority government by international sanctions.

The theory of change used by the ANC was shaped by a Marxist outlook. This was partly informed by its long association with the South African Communist Party, which in 1989 elaborated the concept of 'Colonialism of a Special Type': 'South Africa has a developed capitalist economy. In our country, and wherever it exists, the capitalist mode of production has the same basic characteristics. It is an exploitative system based on the extraction of surplus value from wage labour.'[56]

The deep thinkers within the leadership core of the ANC were heavily influenced by Marx. For Marx, the essential thesis is workers' right to bring their labour to market and to receive fair compensation for that labour. He identified the tendency of capital to want to exploit labour as the antithesis. Marxism is the synthesis of these two driving forces within economies, and specifically focuses on what workers can do politically, socially and economically to protect the value of their labour against the exploitative capitalist class.

Many in the ANC brought Marx's framework of analysis to the problem of race in South Africa. Racism therefore became understood as a systemic disenfranchisement of blacks by whites in order to fulfil white capital's instinct to exploit black labour.

The challenge that these two forms of analysis – the BCM's Hegelian analysis and the ANC's Marxist analysis – pose to leaders is in reconciling Marx's materialism and Hegelian humanism into one vision of the type of society they are trying to create. For the proponents of Black Consciousness, achieving the synthesis of non-racialism means a removal of a racist regime that they previously defined as corrupt, immoral and bullying, and lacking legitimacy and virtue. It also means creating a state that delivers on the desires of indigenous people to feel pride in their beauty, power and virtue.

For many leaders of the ANC, non-racialism is not possible until one removes the core tenets of a racist regime defined as an exploitative capitalist machinery that impedes the rights of work-ers. The consensus reached by ANC leaders in 1994 was that the capitalist machinery is best infiltrated from within rather than destroyed from the outside. This approach necessitated an achieve-ment of synthesis through policies that retain a certain continuity with the race-based categorisation invented by the oppressors. The challenge created by this approach is the added complexity that comes with the promise made by the ANC that the party would deliver changes in the material conditions of all South Africans. How the ANC proposed to reverse 350 years of wealth distribution based on racial categories by keeping the institu-tional system intact was glossed over. In other words, the ANC's definition of a better life for all was for wealth to be distributed in a way that reflects the demographics of the country, but its theory of change was gradualist. Therefore, improvement to the material conditions of black people had to include slowly opening up the capitalist classes for black entrepreneurs. The ANC aimed to enforce this process by taking over the commanding heights of the economy, using political power to redistribute wealth. This objective was never achieved.

As most people who understand the ANC conclude, the organisation is a broad church. Through its gradualist approach to change, the ANC has managed to keep the interests of labour, communists, pragmatists, black nationalists, white conservatives and black business together under one roof. This balancing act was possible when, as the ANC managed to do for the first 95 years of its existence, the organisation retained the moral high ground in society.

The BCM was far less complicated in its composition. It was free to be bold, by virtue of its roots as a student organisation that was home to black intellectuals who were only divided into two camps – idealists and pragmatists. The organisation was run effectively because Steve Biko and Barney Pityana were both idealists with pragmatic leanings, who could at any given time hear the desires of leaders from both sides of the movement. By and large, many of the pragmatic members of the BCM joined the ANC. The idealists, like my mother, opted to stay in the private sector, join civic organisations, become members of the clergy, be part of other political formations or remain public intellectuals.

Because of the ANC's broad-church structure, ideological positions have been routinely traded in exchange for the retention of power and peaceful relations with corporate South Africa. This situation has led to many instances where policy positions taken at ANC policy conferences are ignored by those in government. Over time, as the organisation has grown, leaders in good standing have often taken diametrically opposite positions while claiming to be following through on agreed party policies. These pragmatic political calculations have eroded the party's primary currency – its moral high ground.

As a result, the centre, both in the ANC and in South African society, refuses to hold. South African business feels that it suffers taxation without adequate representation at the seat of ANC power, the National Executive Committee. Labour believes that its constituents' right to a fair wage are being disregarded while business, according to them, gets away with unfair labour practices. Communists, to the extent that they still truly exist within the party, openly question why they have thrown in their lot with an economy run by their comrades according to the Washington Consensus. Black nationalists have reconstituted themselves around the concept of radical economic transformation (RET) as the only way out of the country's quagmire.

To the extent that they are speaking to each other at all, these various factions see reality very differently.

Business feels that it has acquiesced to pressure from government to bring on board black partners with the aim of qualifying for government procurement. This process, called black economic empowerment (BEE), has had mixed results. The chief success of BEE has come from dividends and asset disposals that have resulted in the upliftment of tens of thousands of households.

The accompanying policy of affirmative action in the workplace has helped to moderately transform the South African corporate landscape, resulting in a few million black people earning attractive salaries, which in turn has created a black middle class. This, however, has also created a sense of resentment among the tens of millions of indigenous South Africans who have been left behind.

These two policies, BEE and affirmative action, have perversely served as a unifying factor for many white South Africans, who work together to protect their interests against those seeking to encroach on their dominant positions in the economy.

Many within the ANC feel that BEE has to be replaced by RET. Yet those who have publicly called for RET have been rebuked by industry titans such as Johann Rupert, who believe they are only looking for a policy to justify 'rent-seeking'. This perception is not helped by the fact that many of the loudest proponents of RET are associated with cases of corruption.

Of course, the proponents of RET counter that people like Johann Rupert dislike them because they are determined to keep white monopoly capital intact. A recently released position paper on RET states that 'Radical Economic Transformation (RET) is a programme of action of the African National Congress, whose aim is to initiate a radical second phase of the National Democratic Revolution'.[57] What this document, and other public utterances of those supporting RET, shows is that RET is less a plan than a sentiment, which holds that the time has come for indigenous people to own a significant portion of the economy.

With all of these opposing interests, a level of suspicion and cynicism has befallen ordinary South Africans. They no longer know whom to believe.

President Franklin D Roosevelt once put forward a simple test for the health of a nation. At his second inaugural address, on 20 January 1937, he proclaimed: 'The test of our progress is not whether we add more to the abundance of those who have much; it is whether we provide enough for those that have too little.'[58] I believe Steve Biko would have agreed that this is an accurate test both of a nation's health and of its lived values. Sadly, modern

South Africa has so far failed this test both in fact and in spirit. The huge disparity between the rich and the poor is proof of this. On a spiritual level we are also failing since we do not really seem to grasp and identify with the humiliation suffered by the majority of South Africans, who lack employment opportunities, livelihoods, sustenance and shelter.

Steve Biko offered a goal that our society should aspire to when he said: 'We have set our quest for true humanity, and somewhere on the distant horizon we can see the glittering prize . . . Let us march forth with courage and determination, drawing strength from our common plight and our brotherhood.'[59]

I have no doubt that were he alive today, my father would support the calls for radical economic transformation if, in its implementation, it kept as its north star this quest to win the glittering prize that is true humanity. Biko never yielded in his call for South Africa to belong to South Africans. What would be frustrating to him is for a party that is in power to pass resolutions to effect change and then to completely contradict itself through the actions taken by those it deploys to government.

In the last interview he gave before he was killed, Biko acknowledged the ANC as the vanguard South African liberation organisation. When he made this comment, he no doubt had in mind a different ANC to the one I am a member of today. I believe he would struggle to recognise the current version of the ANC, where leaders routinely buy seats to secure leadership positions, are sometimes paid by business to pass particular laws, are cowed into submission against land restitution without compensation and, a few years ago, declared war on 'clever blacks'. He would not recognise the party that has become known for state capture and other forms of corruption. He would be ashamed of the timidity with which some leaders of the ANC treat white corporate-interest groups.

What would have pained my father the most, though, is the loss of the most valuable commodity any liberation organisation can possess – the moral high ground. The biggest indictment against the ANC is that it cannot credibly call for and enact RET in the face of the shocking inequality in the country.

Of course, it is not true that all ANC leaders are corrupt. There are many committed members of the ANC who are attempting to win back the party from the corrupt elements in its midst. It is certainly not true that RET is a codeword for looting. What is true is that because of rampant corruption and mismanagement, black leadership across the board has lost the credibility to effectively lead society.

In the last ANC election cycle, the most forceful and high-ranking proponent of RET was Nkosazana Dlamini-Zuma. Her campaign for party president was anchored in ideas that she thought would champion RET as the mechanism for broad-based economic redress. That she narrowly lost her campaign for the presidency might be an indication of the level of support RET has within the party.

It says a lot about the influence of the BCM that both leading candidates for the presidency of the ANC were former BCM members. As a student, President Cyril Ramaphosa was the chair of SASO's University of the North branch. He may be a pragmatist today, but during his formative years as a student leader, the BCM philosophy greatly influenced both his style of leadership and his worldview. When he left student politics, his entry into trade union politics allowed him to bolster his political consciousness with a thorough understanding of the plight of black workers.

As president of the ANC, Cyril Ramaphosa has to deal with escalating escalating strife within the party, driven by the formation of a coalition of wounded political veterans of the struggle for freedom, together with young party members who are tired of gradualism. This coalition of the politically wounded vies for control of the broad church that has its members congregated in four corners.

In the one corner are those who argue for more labour-market security for workers, as well as increased salaries as a major transformational tool. In the second corner are black businesses, asking for access to capital and procurement in favour of black-owned businesses. In the third corner are the members of NGOs who are asking for a meritocratic public service that fires workers not able to demonstrate proficiency in their jobs. ANC leaders who are part of big business sit in the fourth corner, in silent or sometimes vocal opposition to labour-union collective-bargaining strategies and preferential government treatment of black-owned and -managed businesses.

The contradictions that emanate from these varying actors and their different objectives have led to policy paralysis and a self-defeating set of government laws and regulations. President Ramaphosa has not helped himself by failing either to wholly accept RET or to set a policy alternative. He seems to have chosen a more measured route, taking from RET those policy positions he likes and bringing forth more moderate alternatives to those RET positions he doesn't like. The result has left him looking weak and indecisive, and consequently politically vulnerable.

If I had to interview the surviving former BCM leaders within the ANC and seek to rank their individual priorities, each person would bring to the table different views on what to do first and what to do last. Policy is not an arena that can sustain unified thought within the broad church that is the ANC. What the BCM leaders who joined the ANC should have done, and can still do, is to make it their business to continue to push for cultural transformation as an alternative change agency. The absence of an independent cultural movement such as the BCM that could serve as a counterweight to the focus on material conditions of the South African Communist Party and the Congress of South African Trade Unions has left an imbalance within the tripartite alliance. The outcome is that compromises that pander to the needs of capital are prioritised over the need to deliver psychological liberation.

What has kept the frustrations of the majority of psychologically oppressed South Africans at bay is the welfare system. Most people in the ANC have been able to agree on the need to create a welfare state through the social-grant system, the provision of free housing and the delivery of free education and subsidised basic services. The challenge the ANC government faces is finding a sustainable economic-growth model to pay for these welfare benefits. In searching for an economically sustainable growth model, they are hampered by some of the policy contradictions I have outlined above. The result is national economic stagnation, weighed down by growing long-term debt.

As the economy flounders, the underlying reality of a psychologically oppressed majority is threatening to tear down the foundations of this house of cards. With no common enemy to unite against, xenophobia has been a short-term outlet for these frustrations. But in the absence of a real enemy, we retreat to our identity politics of old, and find in each other the scapegoats we so desperately need to explain away our failure.

Based on the current political climate, RET versus white mono-poly capital is destined to be the branding of two warring factions that will beat each other into oblivion. This fight will leave little to no room for moderates to keep a sound footing. In anticipation of this fight, the DA has availed itself as an ally of President Cyril Ramaphosa in fighting against the RET faction within his own party. This is an ominous sign for the ANC. These dynamic forces and counterforces drive the party closer and closer to the brink of political combustion. Reconciliation between the two factions is becoming ever more improbable. In the party's search for a way forward, the ANC needs to push back against both corruption and the resurgence of white custodianship sought by the white-monopoly-capital faction.

To illuminate the path to the type of ANC envisioned by Biko, Sobukwe, Hani, Mandela, Sisulu and Tambo as the vanguard of this country, a simple reality must be accepted. Only RET can recon-struct the ownership patterns of the country in a way that effects meaningful change. The debate we should be having, both within the ANC and outside it, is about the type of RET we should be implementing. To get the country to support RET, the party needs to set new, post-Zondo Commission standards of governance that will spell out the accompanying obligations RET brings in the form of fiscal transparency, anti-corruption measures and the cultural transformation that should close the door on our past and allow us to become a forward-looking non-racial nation.

Maturity, integrity and perspective are key to establishing what our needs as a society are, how these needs can cascade down to the level of the individual, and who pays for their attainment. The RET faction of the ANC needs to see why this moment, like 1994, calls for the ANC to produce its most credible leadership as new stewards of economic freedom. White monopoly capital needs to understand that the compromise it can make today, in the form of a once-off financial transfer of wealth, will give business the predictability it seeks in planning for a long-term future.

It is important for all sides to remember that we are still in the very early stages of our history as a nation. According to Hegel's teachings, the early stages of a society's history seldom produce clarity between conflicting ideas. It is not yet possible for us to assess the different possible policy outcomes from trading one thing for another. Weighing the material objectives versus the psychological objectives requires a delicate balancing act.

Experience should teach us that even though we are an interconnected web called a nation, the coherent quality of our ideas, concepts and beliefs at the level of the individual citizen are essential to how the country will look one day. At the level of the individual citizen, what we want may not be that different. We all want to be valued, respected and productive members of society. We all expect that our productivity will be remunerated such that we can have the ability to take care of our families. We all want our children to have better opportunities than we did. These general requirements cross colour, gender and cultural lines.

Our overarching priority should be to build a society that is guided by the delivery of these basic requirements to all South Africans. Our evolving consciousness as a nation must constantly be judged by the ability of our society to retain the dignity of individual citizens. This may sound idealistic, but I can assure you that this is our most pragmatic path to a peaceful South African future. This idealistic pragmatism is a missing ingredient that someone like Steve Biko would have brought to the ANC.

If Tambo and Biko had reached a consensus at their planned meeting in 1977, my father might have gone into exile and spent his energy embedding Black Consciousness more deeply into the thinking of ANC leaders. Steve Biko would have imparted lessons to the ANC leadership in workshops shaped by Paulo Freire's belief that 'one cannot reduce the analysis of racism to social class, and one cannot understand racism fully without class analysis, for to do one at the expense of the other is to fall into a sectarianist position, which is as despicable as the racism that we need to reject'.[60]

To date, the ANC has found it impossible to retain this subtle dialectic balance of ideas as the driving force of its policy positions. Its positions have been heavily skewed at some times by a Marxist, materialist belief system that ignores the human psychological wounds inflicted by apartheid, and at other times by a dogmatic anti-white rhetoric that misses the fact that whiteness as a social category was introduced merely for privilege-preservation purposes. Based on this imbalance, too much emphasis has been placed on BEE as a redistribution mechanism without understanding the need for broad-based human development among black people. Too much emphasis has been placed on the language of race, without focusing on changing the dominant culture in South Africa in order to redefine what non-racialism means.

I believe that if my father were alive today, the ANC would have taken a completely different approach to the human development of young South Africans. Our education system would be based on an African syllabus that would teach the African child all the traditional subjects from an African perspective that is designed to create whole, healed beings who could meaningfully contribute to the reconstruction of our society on their own terms. If Steve Biko were alive, we would have a country that gladly embraces African culture as the dominant driving force for how society is organised, and that would make African languages the default languages spoken by all South Africans. We would dress differently, holiday differently and feel a different way about celebrating who we are.

Such a shift in priorities could possibly have anchored the ANC in a way that would have made its leaders less susceptible to corruption, making the country more willing to accept a drastic shift in economic policy towards RET. My father was not alone in harbouring these beliefs; many current and former ANC leaders share his nuanced understanding of the nexus of class, race, culture and the psychology of the oppressed. What Steve Biko would have brought to the table are the intellectual property and the tools the ANC could have used to embed these teachings in the daily training of its leaders in order that they become second nature. All of us in the country are the poorer for his death.

We are, however, blessed with the wealth of Biko's and many other struggle leaders' wisdom. We only need to invest the time in reading and listening to their sage advice as we seek guidance through what will be the defining decade in South Africa's history.

Notes

2 An oasis of excellence

1. Steve Biko, *I Write What I Like: 40th Anniversary Edition* (Johannesburg: Picador Africa, 2017).

3 A lioness at the foot of the Soutpansberg

2. Biko, *I Write What I Like*.

4 The 'Durban Moment'

3. These four points are based on 'Steve Biko Speaks! Black Consciousness and the South African Revolution', audio interview, August 1977. YouTube, 11 June 2015. See www.youtube.com/watch?v = Q25It5kMexg.
4. Daniel Magaziner, 'Interview with Strini Moodley', Aluka, 2006. See psimg. jstor.org/fsi/img/pdf/t0/10.5555/al.sff.document.magazp1b1006_final.pdf (limited access).
5. Ibid.
6. Ibid.
7. Amy Jacques-Garvey (ed), Philosophy and Opinions of Marcus Garvey, ebook (Ravenio Books, 2015).
8. South African History Online, 'University Christian Movement', 27 August 2019. See www.sahistory.org.za/article/university-christian-movement-ucm.
9. Biko, *I Write What I Like*.
10. Ibid.
11. Barney Pityana, Mamphela Ramphele, Malusi Mpumlwana and Lindy Wilson, *Bounds of Possibility: The Legacy of Steve Biko and Black Consciousness* (Cape Town: David Philip, 1991).
12. Biko, *I Write What I Like*.

5 A movement is born

13. Biko, S and Millard, AW (ed.). No Fears Expressed: Quotes From Steve Biko.(Johannesburg: Pan Macmillan, 2017).
14. Biko, *I Write What I Like*.

6 Faith and faithlessness

15. Jacques-Garvey (ed), *Philosophy and Opinions of Marcus Garvey*.
16. Sigqibo Dwane, 'Christianity in Relation to Xhosa Religion', PhD dissertation, University of London, 1979.
17. James H Cone, *Black Theology and Black Power* (Maryknoll, NY: Orbis Books, 1997).
18. Biko, *I Write What I Like*.
19. Martin Luther King, Jr, 'Loving Your Enemies', sermon delivered at Dexter Avenue Baptist Church, 17 November 1957. The Martin Luther King, Jr, Research and Education Institute, Stanford University. See kinginstitute.stanford.edu/king-papers/documents/loving-your-enemies-sermon-delivered-dexter-avenue-baptist-church.
20. Malcolm X, 'Racial Separation', speech at University of California at Berkeley, 11 October 1963. See www.blackpast.org/african-american-history/speeches-african-american-history/1963-malcolm-x-racial-separation/.
21. Stokely Carmichael, 'Black Power', speech, 29 October 1966. Voices of Democracy: The US Oratory Project, University of Maryland. See voicesofdemocracy.umd.edu/carmichael-black-power-speech-text/.
22. Cited in Rufus Burrow, Jr, 'James H Cone: Father of Contemporary Black Theology', *The Asbury Theological Journal* vol 48, no 2 (1993): 59–75.
23. Cited in Malesela John Lamola, 'The Thought of Steve Biko as the Historico-Philosophical Base of South African Black Theology', *Journal of Black Theology* vol 3, no 2 (November 1989).

7 Harnessing the power of ubuntu

24. Paulo Freire, *Pedagogy of the Oppressed* (London: Continuum, 1968).
25. Ibid.
26. Ibid.
27. South African History Online, 'Black Community Programmes (BCP)', 27 August 2019. See www.sahistory.org.za/article/black-community-programmes-bcp.

28. Mafika Pascal Gwala (ed), 'Chapter one: Self-help', *Black Review 1973*. See disa. ukzn.ac.za/Br19730376435400000019743.

29. South African History Online, 'Black Community Programmes (BCP)'.

8 An unjust trial and unjustifiable murders

30. Sumboornam Moodley (ed), *Time to Remember: Reflections of Women From the Black Consciousness Movement* (Durban: Women for Awareness, 2018).

31. Millard Arnold (ed), *Steve Biko: Black Consciousness in South Africa* (New York: Vintage Books, 1979).

32. Ibid.

33. Ibid.

9 Sprout

34. Arnold (ed), *Steve Biko: Black Consciousness in South Africa*.

35. 'Judge Speechless at Rodrigues Court Appearance', press release, 6 May 2021. Ahmed Timol: Truth Prevails. See www.ahmedtimol.co.za/judge-speechless-at-rodrigues-court-appearance/.

10 Born at the right time

36. World Health Organization, 'South Africa: Alcohol Consumption and Patterns', factsheet, 2018. See www.who.int/substance_abuse/publications/global_alcohol_report/profiles/zaf.pdf?ua=1.

37. The South African Depression and Anxiety Group, 'SA's sick state of mental health', article from the *Sunday Times*, 6 July 2014. See www.sadag.org/index.php?option=com_content&view=article&id=2178:sa-s-sick-state-of-mental-health&catid=74&Itemid=132.

38. Jacques-Garvey (ed), *Philosophy and Opinions of Marcus Garvey*.

11 Pale skin, white masks

39. Arnold (ed), *Steve Biko: No Fears Expressed*.

40. Ann Gibbons, 'How Europeans evolved white skin', *Science*, 2 April 2015. See www.sciencemag.org/news/2015/04/how-europeans-evolved-white-skin.

41. Hlumelo Biko, *Africa Reimagined: Reclaiming a Sense of Abundance and Prosperity* (Johannesburg: Jonathan Ball Publishers, 2019).

42. Neville Alexander, 'Racial Identity, Citizenship and Nation Building in Post-Apartheid South Africa', lecture given at East London Campus, University of Fort Hare, 25 March 2006. See www.marxists.org/archive/alexander/2006-racial-identity-citizenship-and-nation-building.pdf.

43. Constitution of the Republic of South Africa, 1996, Act 108 of 1996, Chapter 1, Section 1 (a).
44. Biko, *I Write What I Like*.
45. Steve Biko, 'White Racism and Black Consciousness', 1st Inter-University Workshop on Students and Youth in South Africa, Abe Bailey Institute of Inter-Racial Studies, University of Cape Town, 1971.
46. Arnold (ed), *Steve Biko: No Fears Expressed*.
47. Biko, *I Write What I Like*.
48. Mamphela Ramphele, *Conversations with My Sons and Daughters* (Johannesburg: Penguin Random House, 2012).
49. Biko, *I Write What I Like*.
50. Ibid.
51. Paul Tillich, *The Courage to Be*, 2nd edition (New Haven and London: Yale University Press, 2000).
52. Department of Labour, 'Employment and Labour on 20th Commission for Employment Equity (CEE) Annual Report', 19 August 2020. See www.gov.za/speeches/employment-and-labur-20th-commission-employment-equity-cee-annual-report-2019%E2%80%9320-19-aug#.

12 The BCM within the ANC

53. James de Villiers, 'Former DA leader Tony Leon: "Checking your privilege is absolute garbage"', *News24*, 3 April 2021.
54. Freire, *Pedagogy of the Oppressed*.
55. Biko, *I Write What I Like*.
56. South African Communist Party, 'Colonialism of a Special Type', section 3 of 'The Path to Power', the programme of the South African Communist Party, as adopted at the Seventh Congress, 1989. See omalley.nelsonmandela.org/omalley/index.php/site/q/03lv02424/04lv02730/05lv03005/06lv03132/07lv03140.htm.
57. Carl Niehaus, 'The RET manifesto', Politicsweb, 15 March 2021. See www.politicsweb.co.za/documents/the-ret-manifesto.
58. 'January 20, 1937: Second Inaugural Address', transcript of speech given by President Franklin Delano Roosevelt. Miller Center, University of Virginia. See millercenter.org/the-presidency/presidential-speeches/january-20-1937-second-inaugural-address.
59. Biko, *I Write What I Like*.
60. Freire, *Pedagogy of the Oppressed*.

Sources

Alexander, Neville. 'Racial Identity, Citizenship and Nation Building in Post-Apartheid South Africa'. Lecture given at East London Campus, University of Fort Hare, 25 March 2006. See www.marxists.org/archive/alexander/2006-racial-identity-citizenship-and-nation-building.pdf.

Arnold, Millard (ed). *Steve Biko: Black Consciousness in South Africa*. New York: Vintage Books, 1979.

Biko, Hlumelo. *Africa Reimagined: Reclaiming a Sense of Abundance and Prosperity*. Johannesburg: Jonathan Ball Publishers, 2019.

Biko, S and Millard, AW (ed.). No Fears Expressed: Quotes From Steve Biko. Johannesburg: Pan Macmillan, 2017.

Biko, Steve. *I Write What I Like: 40th Anniversary Edition*. Johannesburg: Picador Africa, 2017.

—. 'White Racism and Black Consciousness'. 1st Inter-University Workshop on Students and Youth in South Africa, Abe Bailey Institute of Inter-Racial Studies, University of Cape Town, 1971.

Burrow, Rufus, Jr. 'James H Cone: Father of Contemporary Black Theology'. *The Asbury Theological Journal* vol 48, no 2 (1993): 59–75.

Carmichael, Stokely. 'Black Power'. Speech, 29 October 1966. Voices of Democracy: The US Oratory Project, University of Maryland. See voicesofdemocracy.umd.edu/carmichael-black-power-speech-text/.

Cone, James H. *Black Theology and Black Power*. Maryknoll, NY: Orbis Books 1997.

Constitution of the Republic of South Africa, 1996, Act 108 of 1996.

Department of Labour. 'Employment and Labour on 20th Commission for Employment Equity (CEE) Annual Report', 19 August 2020. See www.gov.

za/speeches/employment-and-labur-20th-commission-employment-equity-
cee-annual-report-2019%E2%80%9320-19-aug#.

De Villiers, James. 'Former DA leader Tony Leon: "Checking your privilege is
absolute garbage"'. *News24*, 3 April 2021.

Dwane, Sigqibo. 'Christianity in Relation to Xhosa Religion'. PhD dissertation,
University of London, 1979.

Freire, Paulo. *Pedagogy of the Oppressed*. London: Continuum, 1968.

Gibbons, Ann. 'How Europeans evolved white skin'. *Science*, 2 April 2015. See
www.sciencemag.org/news/2015/04/how-europeans-evolved-white-skin.

Gwala, Mafika Pascal (ed). 'Chapter one: Self-help'. *Black Review 1973*. See
disa.ukzn.ac.za/Br19730376435400000019743.

Jacques-Garvey, Amy (ed). *Philosophy and Opinions of Marcus Garvey* (ebook).
Ravenio Books, 2015.

'January 20, 1937: Second Inaugural Address'. Transcript of speech given by
President Franklin Delano Roosevelt. Miller Center, University of Virginia.
See millercenter.org/the-presidency/presidential-speeches/janu-
ary-20-1937-second-inaugural-address.

'Judge Speechless at Rodrigues Court Appearance'. Press release, 6 May 2021.
Ahmed Timol: Truth Prevails. See www.ahmedtimol.co.za/judge-speechless-
at-rodrigues-court-appearance/.

King, Martin Luther, Jr. 'Loving Your Enemies'. Sermon delivered at
Dexter Avenue Baptist Church, 17 November 1957. The Martin Luther
King, Jr, Research and Education Institute, Stanford University. See
kinginstitute.stanford.edu/king-papers/documents/loving-your-ene-
mies-sermon-delivered-dexter-avenue-baptist-church.

Lamola, Malesela John. 'The Thought of Steve Biko as the Historico-
Philosophical Base of South African Black Theology'. *Journal of Black
Theology* vol 3, no 2 (November 1989).

Magaziner, Daniel. 'Interview with Strini Moodley', Aluka, 2006. See
psimg.jstor.org/fsi/img/pdf/t0/10.5555/al.sff.document.magazp1b1006_
final.pdf (limited access).

Malcolm X. 'Racial Separation'. Speech at University of California at Berkeley,
11 October 1963. See www.blackpast.org/african-american-history/speeches-
african-american-history/1963-malcolm-x-racial-separation/.

Moodley, Sumboornam (ed). *Time to Remember: Reflections of Women From the
Black Consciousness Movement*. Durban: Women for Awareness, 2018.

Niehaus, Carl. 'The RET manifesto'. Politicsweb, 15 March 2021. See www.politicsweb.co.za/documents/the-ret-manifesto.

Pityana, Barney, Mamphela Ramphele, Malusi Mpumlwana and Lindy Wilson. *Bounds of Possibility: The Legacy of Steve Biko and Black Consciousness.* Cape Town: David Philip, 1991.

Ramphele, Mamphela. *Conversations with My Sons and Daughters.* Johannesburg: Penguin Random House, 2012.

South African Communist Party. 'Colonialism of a Special Type'. Section 3 of 'The Path to Power', the programme of the South African Communist Party, as adopted at the Seventh Congress, 1989. See omalley.nelsonmandela.org/omalley/index.php/site/q/03lv02424/04lv02730/05lv03005/06lv03132/07lv03140.htm.

South African History Online. 'Black Community Programmes (BCP)', 27 August 2019. See www.sahistory.org.za/article/black-community-programmes-bcp.

—. 'University Christian Movement', 27 August 2019. See www.sahistory.org.za/article/university-christian-movement-ucm.

The South African Depression and Anxiety Group. 'SA's sick state of mental health'. Article from the *Sunday Times*, 6 July 2014. See www.sadag.org/index.php?option = com_content&view = article&id = 2178:sa-s-sick-state-of-mental-health&catid = 74&Itemid = 132.

'Steve Biko Speaks! Black Consciousness and the South African Revolution'. Audio interview, August 1977. See www.youtube.com/watch?v = Q25It5k-Mexg.

Tillich, Paul. *The Courage to Be.* 2nd edition. New Haven and London: Yale University Press, 2000.

World Health Organization. 'South Africa: Alcohol Consumption and Patterns'. Factsheet, 2018. See www.who.int/substance_abuse/publications/global_alcohol_report/profiles/zaf.pdf?ua = 1.

Acknowledgements

There are many people who have helped me to tell this story, and I wish to thank them for their contributions. My interviews with, in particular, Barney Pityana, Mamphela Ramphele, Charles Sibisi, Malusi Mpumlwana and Saths Cooper allowed me to tap into their deep insights and wisdom on the genesis and development of Black Consciousness.

In writing this book I have been greatly helped by Annie Olivier of Jonathan Ball Publishers. Her rigour and dedication have enriched the result immeasurably. Thanks also to editor Alfred LeMaitre, for his close attention to detail, and to designer Nazli Jacobs.

I also wish to acknowledge the innumerable contributions to my life made by my grandmothers Tsipu and Mamcete, by my uncles Sethiba, Malesela, Mathabatha, Ramphele and Molepo, by my aunts Mashadi, Luna, Nontlungu and Bukelwa, and by Uncle Khaya, my father, Bantu, and Aunt Bandi.

Index

Note: page numbers in *italics* indicate a photograph.

www.ingramcontent.com/pod-product-compliance
Lightning Source LLC
Chambersburg PA
CBHW050648270326
41927CB00012B/2929